Atonement

EDITED BY

GABRIEL N. E. FLUHRER

PUBLISHING
P.O. BOX 817 • PHILLIPSBURG • NEW JERSEY 08865-0817

Unless otherwise indicated, Scripture quotations are from *ESV Bible*® (*The Holy Bible, English Standard Version*®). Copyright © 2001 by Crossway Bibles, a publishing ministry of Good News Publishers. Used by permission. All rights reserved.

Italics within Scripture quotations indicate emphasis added.

Printed in the United States of America

Library of Congress Cataloging-in-Publication Data

Atonement / edited by Gabriel N.E. Fluhrer.
    p. cm.
  Includes index.
  ISBN 978-1-59638-178-0 (pbk.)
  1. Atonement. 2. Reformed Church--Doctrines. I. Fluhrer, Gabriel N. E., 1978-
  BT265.3.A85 2010
  234'.5--dc22
                       2009047291

To the students of Second Presbyterian Church,

with the prayer that they will always glory in the wonder of the atonement.

Contents

Editor's Preface

*Nothing can for sin atone, nothing but the blood
of Jesus; naught of good that I have done—nothing
but the blood of Jesus!*[1]

THIS IS A BOOK about blood and it soaks every page. Our culture generally accepts that spilled blood is a part of life, and without protest, we watch horror movies, medical and crime dramas, the news, and even live births. But when blood is joined with the word *atonement*, we often get squeamish, and our tolerance transforms into disgust and hostility. Thankfully, God will not lighten his claim upon his creatures on account of their weakness.

Christian theology has always understood atonement as the "reparation for an offense or injury"[2] as it applies to the relationship between God and man. We offend God, and Christ makes reparation for our offense. Christians understand that God graciously has provided a way to be right with him only

---

1. "Nothing But the Blood." Words and music: Robert Lowry, 1876.
2. *Merriam-Webster Online Dictionary*, s.v. "Atonement," http://www.merriam-webster.com/dictionary/atonement (accessed August 31, 2009).

by means of the atonement that Jesus Christ made on a Roman cross nearly two thousand years ago.

Today, along with other great doctrines of the Christian faith, the doctrine of the blood atonement of Christ is under attack. It is derided as "cosmic child abuse" and traded for a grandfatherly sentimentalism that muffles the piercing cries of the Savior being nailed to the cross. The pride of our sin dilutes the simple, clear, and shocking teaching of the New Testament: God killed his perfect Son to save hate-filled rebels from the wrath they deserve. The doctrine of blood atonement makes God too personal, too sovereign, and too violent for modern people who prefer Oprah's "non-judgmental god stuff," to use her words. For this reason, I have compiled the words of the following authors into one volume. These men love the atonement and they believe in its beautiful truth so strongly that they can't help but preach it.

The elder statesman, J.I. Packer, begins with the necessity of the atonement. His section on sin is alone worth the price of the book. Dr. John de Witt follows with the nature of the atonement as it relates to reconciliation between condemned sinners and a holy God. Next, the late Dr. James M. Boice further discusses the nature of the atonement, specifically as it relates to a word that is no longer used in common speech: *propitiation*. We can only pray that his essay will inspire us to recover this precious and thoroughly biblical truth.

Following Dr. Boice is the late Dr. John Gerstner. If anyone could explain God's purpose for the atonement, it was this man. Point your friends who question Reformed theology to Dr. Gerstner's essay first. Dr. R.C. Sproul, Dr. Gerstner's protégé, (and a mentor to so many of us through his books and radio shows) then speaks about the themes of sacrifice and satisfaction in relation to the atonement. Put simply, it is vintage Sproul. Dr. Boice returns with a brilliant piece on the atonement and redemption, followed by Dr. Sinclair Ferguson on Christ as our sin-bearer. Both of these chapters give us these two fathers of the faith at their best.

The closing chapter by Dr. Alistair Begg is one of the finest arguments I've ever read or heard for why we must preach the cross. Many readers may be tempted to think that this portion applies only to those called to be pastors, but this would be a mistake. Dr. Begg challenges all who love the cross to preach it, regardless of their role in the church.

I have many more people to thank than space and time will allow. Let me quickly mention a few.

To Mr. Bob Brady and the Alliance of Confessing Evangelicals, and to Marvin Padgett, Aaron Gottier, Nick Darrell, and the good folks at P&R, thank you for giving me this awesome and humbling task. I cannot express my gratitude enough; it has been pure joy.

To my pastor, mentor, and co-laborer, Rev. Richard D. Phillips, I can only say that it is a privilege to serve with you and see what the atonement rightly preached, prayed, and pastored does for a local church. You are "the one in one thousand."

To my other pastor, mentor, and co-worker, Rev. Robert E. Spears, again, I can only express the deepest gratitude for your love, care, and awesome endurance in the midst of trial. The lives changed by the Lord through you will be known on that great day.

To the congregation, staff, and session of Second Presbyterian Church, thank you for your patience with a young pastor, your love of his family, and the constant support and care of me since my acceptance of Christ. I love all of you and bless the Lord for you.

To my dear wife—an answer to prayer, a forgiving helpmate, and a woman of grace—I love you and know that my debt to you and your love is beyond measure. Also, to my precious little Garner, may you, in time, know and rejoice in the atonement.

Finally, saving the best for last, to my Lord, Savior, righteousness, wrath quencher, and King, Jesus, thank you for taking a wretch and allowing him to understand the wonder of your work on his behalf. I exalt in the triune God of my salvation, to whom alone belong riches, honor, glory, and power, now and forevermore.

At a time when the atonement is considered at best an embarrassment and, at worst, a disgusting barbarism, here are men who think of neither. These men have been saved by the atonement and they offer it as a feast that neither summons sinners to do what they cannot do alone, nor asks them to shrink back from a world that has and will always hate the one message that alone can save it.

The table is set to feast, not on platitudes or tired speculations, but on the solid food of cross-saturated thinking. It has been an incalculable and soul-gratifying pleasure to set it for you. Feast on and rejoice in the only true wonder that is left of the ancient world, the wondrous, bloody cross. May it never disgust you but only delight.

Gabriel N. E. Fluhrer

1

The Necessity of the Atonement

J. I. PACKER

He who did not spare his own Son but gave him up for us all, how will he not also with him graciously give us all things? —Romans 8:32

WHAT A MAGNIFICENT statement we find in the eighth chapter of Paul's letter to the Romans. The tremendous assurance it expresses is an incomparable privilege to those who can take it with them through life and into eternity. As we stand at the foot of this great mountain peak of a text, we must gain our footing and understand the journey that has led us to such a majestic crag. In particular, we must focus on verse 32, which gives glorious assurance and comes at the heart of the climactic conclusion of Romans 8, the Everest of the New Testament and a high peak of all biblical writing.

Romans 8 is a rhapsody on assurance that amplifies chapter 5:1–11, Paul's first statement of Christian assurance in this letter, which begins and ends as follows: "Therefore, since we have been justified by faith, we have peace with God through our Lord Jesus Christ. . . . We also rejoice in God through our Lord Jesus Christ, through whom we have now received reconciliation."

After this first passage on the assurance that God gives to the justified, Paul discusses the Christian life. This is found most explicitly in Romans 7:7, where he asks, "What then shall we say? That the law is sin?" thereby pinpointing the relationship between the law and sin. Paul answers that question in the second half of Romans 7, by giving a most poignant testimony to his own experience as a Christian, saying in effect, "My reach after perfect obedience to the God whose law is good exceeds my grasp. And so I aim at holiness, and again and again fall short." He sums up this dilemma in 7:22–23: "For I delight in the law of God, in my inner being, but I see in my members another law waging war against the law of my mind and making me captive to the law of sin that dwells in my members." He didn't enjoy saying that because he really did delight in the law of God in his inner being. Paul would happily have given his hands and his feet to be able to achieve perfect obedience to the law of God. He would have given anything to be able to encompass that, but he couldn't do it. And the plain statement that he couldn't do it is given in order to show that there is nothing sinful about the law. Paul, however, does connect the law which forbids sin (which simultaneously stirs up sin in him so that his reach after righteousness always exceeds his grasp) and, on the other hand, his actual achievement.

After Paul acknowledges what was true of him, he acknowledges that the same is true of every other Christian. He cries out from his heart in terms that he is sure will issue from every other Christian's heart as well: "Wretched man that I am! Who will deliver me from this body of death?" (Rom. 7:24). He then quickly answers his own question (for, of course, he knows the answer) in verse 25: "Thanks be to God through Jesus Christ our Lord!" Notice that the answer is in the future tense just as the question was.

The situation described in the second half of Romans 7 leaves Paul (and his readers) miserable. There's no joy in reflecting on your reach exceeding your grasp, causing you to acknowledge, day by day, "I aimed at perfection and I didn't make it. I have fallen short. Forgive me my trespasses dear Lord." After remembering what it is that the law tells us about ourselves—namely, that we aren't the righteous persons that we ought to be—Paul now wants to restate the substance of Christian assurance. We weren't righteous before we became Christians, and we still are not even as Christians. But Paul isn't going to let the law get the last word, so to speak, and lock us into the sadness that comes from thinking of moral inadequacy, failure, and shortcoming. Paul now intends to restore our assurance by reminding us of what the gospel says about us. The gospel must have the last word in the Christian's assurance and Paul makes sure that it does. Chapter 8 begins with the liberating promise of no condemnation and ends with the promise of no separation from the love of Christ; the blessings that belongs to those who are in Christ.

To be in Christ is a precious relationship and has several levels of meaning. Very simply, it means that you, by faith, unite yourself to him, come to him, and embrace him from the human side. Behind it all stands the precious doctrine of election by God's eternal choice. And in between the two great promises that this relationship affords, Paul has celebrated adoption, new life, the hope of glory, and strength for our weakness. In short, he has looked at, from every standpoint, the certainty of our being kept in grace until finally we are brought to glory. That is the theme of this great final paragraph and the peroration of the whole passage.

Let us now look at four propositions found in Romans 8 that can be inferred from the hope that flows from justification. The first proposition is that no opposition can succeed against us: "If God is for us, who can be against us?" (Rom. 8:31). Many can try to oppose us, but none can succeed. Not man, and not Satan.

Skipping proposition two momentarily, proposition three is that no accusation can stand against us: "Who shall bring any charge against God's elect? It is God who justifies. Who is to condemn? Christ Jesus is the one who died—more than that, who was raised—who is at the right hand of God, who indeed is interceding for us" (Rom. 8:33–34). If any should appear before the throne of God—even Satan himself—to accuse us of being unfit for the kingdom, God will simply send him away. God, by his grace, is bringing us to his kingdom and he has secured our justification. He has pronounced an "eschatological verdict," which simply means that the verdict belonging to the final judgment has been brought forward in time and pronounced now, so that you and I may rejoice and face that final judgment with the assurance of justification. We are already accepted and nothing can ever change that. That's tremendous, isn't it?

Also tremendous is the assurance found in proposition four, which closes the chapter and promises that nothing in creation will be able to separate us from the love of God that is in Christ Jesus our Lord: "Who shall separate us from the love of Christ?" (Rom. 8:35). Nothing and nobody can ever do it.

Paul ends the chapter on a tremendously high note of certainty and assurance.

Let us now return to proposition two, which I made my final point because it is the focus of what I want to discuss. The argument of proposition two is that since God has already done the greatest thing imaginable to benefit us, we can be 100 percent certain that every lesser benefit of salvation through the death of Christ will be given us: "He who did not spare his own Son but gave him up for us all, how will he not also with him graciously give us all things?" (Rom. 8:32). Those lesser benefits (if we can even call them that) will cost the Father less than our justification cost him. To justify us, he had to give his Son to endure the agony of Calvary's cross. If he did that to save us, we can be sure that every good thing that he can envisage or we can conceive will be given to us as well.

This colossal fourfold assurance that we have found in the final paragraph of Romans 8 is the Himalayan range of Scripture with Romans 8:32 as perhaps its highest peak. The point that we must get clear on is that all of this assurance, salvation, and glory, which is ours now in foretaste and will one day be ours in fullness, comes to us only through the cross of Christ. Given this great fact, the most marvelous thing in God's creation, the most wonderful thing in world history, is that God loved sinners and sent his Son to save them.

I am simply saying, as loudly and as clearly as I can, that everything rests on the atonement. Without Calvary, we would not have hope of escaping the hell that we truly deserve. We have fallen short of the glory of God and lived our lives, more or less, in obedience to sin. We wish God didn't exist so that we could be at the center of the universe, and, accordingly, we try to live that lie as if it were the truth. Christ's death is the springboard for everything that's said about salvation in the book of Romans.

We need to understand the necessity of that death in order to grasp its glory and begin to appreciate its wonder. I strongly believe that the glory of the atonement begins here, but frankly I didn't always see it as clearly as I do now.

Once upon a time, I went to visit a friend at Reformed Theological Seminary in Jackson, Mississippi, in the days when Dr. John R. de Witt was professor of theology. One day my friend asked me if I had any interest to listen to Dr. de Witt teach. I was indeed interested, so we quietly slipped into his classroom and sat down on the back row. I didn't know Dr. de Witt then as well as I do now, but he seemed to recognize me as I entered the classroom. He was lecturing on this subject of the necessity of the atonement, and without prior warning, he introduced me to the class and asked if I had anything to contribute to the topic.

Frankly, I don't enjoy recounting this particular event. What did I do with Dr de Witt's kind recognition and question? I sat on the fence. As far as I know, my motive was good; I didn't want to disrupt any of the impressions that he might have been giving or speak against anything that he might have said. But we never serve God well by simply playing it safe and evading issues. That's what I did and I wish, in retrospect, I hadn't.

My exact answer was something along the lines of, "Well, Reformed theologians have always been divided about this; there have been two views." As Fanny, the woman who was Ebenezer Scrooge's young love interest in *A Christmas Carol* exclaimed, "What a safe and terrible answer!" Let me explain to you in detail what I meant.

Both views assume the basic wonder of God's grace, namely, that he resolves to save sinners. The first view has tremendous support for it and can claim Augustine in the fifth century, Thomas Aquinas in the thirteenth century, a sentence in John

Calvin's writing in the sixteenth century, Samuel Rutherford (who wrote those wonderful letters) in the seventeenth century, and in more recent times, the great Dutchman, Herman Bavinck. All argued for the necessity of the cross and the atonement but called it relative, hypothetical, or conditional. According to this view, the atonement depended on a further decision of God to save those whom he had resolved to save in this way, as distinct from doing it any other way. Those who take this view talk as if it was in God's power to save his elect by some means other than the substitutionary, sin-bearing atonement of Calvary, but in fact, he chose to do it this way.

The second and opposing view possesses equally impressive support. In the seventeenth century, giants like John Owen, the English Puritan, and Francis Turretin took this view. In the past century, the towering Louis Berkhof also took this second view. And all of these theologians looked back to Anselm and his epoch-making work on the atonement from the eleventh century, *Cur Deus Homo*, or *Why did God Become Man?*, in which he argued that the necessity of the atonement was absolute. Anselm and these other great men believed that if God once resolved to save guilty sinners, then this way of Calvary was the only way he could do it. The marvel of Calvary is that God's love, wisdom, and righteousness all met together there. Those three aspects of God's holy character met together at Calvary, and this explains the necessity of the atonement.

It's sad to look back on that little episode in Dr. de Witt's classroom. It was a very poor performance on my part, and I really am ashamed of it. I ought not to have had any doubt about which was the true view, just as the fellows on the wrong side ought not to have had any doubt either because Romans 8:32 is so clear. Paul says that God did not spare his own Son. That language points to the certainty that this was an appallingly costly venture on the part of God the Father. If he could have spared his own Son and still redeemed, we may be sure he would have. God doesn't make needless gestures. The Father's sacrifice of the Son tells us, as sure as eggs are eggs (as we used to say back in England), that it had to be done this way. Our redemption couldn't be achieved at any lesser cost. If the gesture had been needless, it wouldn't have been a wonderful display of love. The glory of Calvary as the demonstration of God's love would be like a punctured balloon. If it were not necessary, then there is nothing wonderful about it after all.

James Denney, a Scottish writer of the past, while in the process of refuting the view of the atonement held by Abelard[1] in the early thirteenth century (Abelard was arguing against Anselm's view), pictured it in the following way: Suppose I am sitting on the pier in the sunshine, on a seaside holiday. While I am sitting there enjoying the sunshine, a man rushes up to me and says, "Look, I'll show you how much I love you!" and then jumps off the end of the pier and is drowned. Denny argued that this wasn't a display of love but rather a display of idiocy! It doesn't mean anything. It's only a display of love if the person who gives his life is doing something for me that had to be done to save me and that I couldn't do for myself.[2]

This is what the New Testament says about Calvary, and, therefore, it is a wonderful demonstration of love. Had it been a needless gesture, there would have been no force behind Paul's conclusion in Romans 8:32: "How will he not also with him graciously give us all things?" You couldn't be certain of the latter promise if God's former action had been foolish and had caused

---

1. Abelard had said that the cross reveals the love of God and then went on to deny that the cross actually was the necessary act of God for putting away the sins of those whom he loved.

2. James Denney, *The Death of Christ* (London: Hodder & Stoughton, 1951), 103.

unnecessary suffering to himself. Paul doesn't seem to allow for that possibility according to his cry of praise: "Oh, the depth of the riches and wisdom and knowledge of God!" (Rom. 11:33). Paul knew better than Abelard and the very phrasing of verse 32 indicates clearly that our salvation had to be accomplished through the sacrifice of the Son or it couldn't be done at all.

Thus, the greatest sacrifice ever was offered. The greatest gesture of love ever was made. He spared not his own Son but gave him up for us all. The New Testament always measures the love of God by the greatness of God's gift of Christ to die on Calvary. When I talk about the necessity of the atonement these days, I wince inside as I remember sitting on the fence in Dr. de Witt's classroom. I speak about the matter very strongly because I believe that I've seen something that I missed before and I don't want anyone else to miss it. To affirm that the necessity of the atonement is basic to the glory of the atonement, I will answer two questions that verse 32 directly prompts. These questions belong together and the answer is clear and far-reaching in both cases.

The first question is whether or not the atonement was necessary. Why couldn't God just forget sin like the liberals are always saying he can? We do that often enough when we are dealing with someone who has done us harm, but later comes and honestly apologizes, showing genuine sorrow for what they did. We say, "Let bygones be bygones!" We simply forgive and leave the matter there. "Why couldn't God do that?" ask the liberals. "Is God less than man?"

The Scriptures very plainly answer this question by saying God couldn't simply let bygones be bygones because the judgment of sin was necessary. And the judgment of sin was necessary because God has a moral nature and a moral character that made it necessary. God cares for the difference between right

9

and wrong in the way that he does because he is a God whom Scripture describes as holy and just. God, therefore, must judge sin because it is in his nature. He must reject sin, show his displeasure at sin, punish sin, and inflict on sin the retribution it deserves. When we talk about the necessary judgment of God, this is the idea that we are expressing.

Now, God doesn't exact judgment for arbitrary reasons, thereby doing something that he didn't have to do, as I argued earlier. He doesn't do it simply for policy reasons to make an impression on people, as Abelard mistakenly supposed. He does it because of the necessity that arises within his own Being. He is the sort of Being and the sort of God who must judge sin and we can see this truth in the Scriptures. But apart from what the Bible tells us, we really don't know anything of the awful nature of sin and the awful holiness of God. If we forget that we really don't know anything, we are kidding ourselves.

The ultimate mistake of liberal theology is to suppose that man is capable of judging God's self-revelation in Scripture and reconstructing what the Bible says in light of man's spiritual "wisdom." This is sheer nonsense. It is the fundamental mistake that produces the many specific mistakes of liberal theology. I beg you to recognize that apart from the light of God's Word, we are in darkness concerning spiritual realities. Humble your mind and prepare yourself to listen to and take seriously what the Bible says.

I start by reminding you of what the Bible says about the nature of sin. We use the word with a merely social meaning. We use it to signify certain types of behavior acted out by one human being against another. This is a bad start because we are secularizing a theological word whose meaning in Scripture is always conceived and defined in terms of a wrong relationship to God. God is the reference point for defining sin, not other humans. The Scripture goes further and tells us how God sees sin. It's God's view of sin that is given in the Bible and that we must adopt.

John Owen, the great Puritan of whom I spoke earlier, in his monumental work on sin, wrote a paragraph in which he summarizes God's view of sin. Read with care the words that Owen used to describe how the creature acts towards his Creator: disgrace, fraud, blasphemy, enmity, hatred, contempt, rebellion and injury, poison, stench, dung, vomit, polluted blood, plague, pestilence, abominable, and detestable. Sin is essentially the resolve—the mad, utterly blameworthy, but nonetheless, utterly firm resolve—to play God and fight the real God. Sinners resolve to treat themselves as the center of the universe and so they keep God at bay on the outer circumference of their lives—or so they think. They won't allow the Creator to rule over them as he wills to do. If they appeal to God at all, they ask God to act according to their will and for their convenience like a servant who gets them out of trouble and bestows on them good gifts. They never serve him from the heart and only resent the claim to dominion that he makes. This is why people like Luther, Calvin, and Owen say, roundly and without question, that sin wills the fundamental abolition of God. Sin wills that God should not be there. Sin plays God, sin fights God, and sin wishes that God didn't exist at all.

It should be easy to see that this attitude produces a monstrous guilt. This is a horror in God's world, and the Bible treats sin as horrible. One of the ways in which sin is presented to us in Scripture (and the references are too great for the space allowed) is as uncleanness. In English, we have a four-letter word for this: dirt. You probably cannot help recoiling at something dirty. Think of your reaction if you were asked to sleep on obviously dirty sheets or to eat your lunch off obviously dirty plates.

Similarly, God cannot help recoiling from that attitude in man that expresses itself in fighting him, defying him, and willing him out of existence. You cannot wonder that he hates the abominations which sin produces. God is holy. Sin is uncleanness in his eyes and he hates it.

Then again, Scripture also says God is just. This means God does everything right and deals rightly with everyone. God expresses his justice by dealing with sin as sin ought to be dealt with. Doesn't your own conscience tell you, and hasn't it always told you that when you've done wrong you ought to be punished? Denney, of whom I spoke earlier, once declared that the most universal experience is a bad conscience. Everybody knows that condemnation of conscience of which Denney was thinking. Conscience doesn't always register by God's standards, but in telling us that sin—our wrongdoing recognized as wrongdoing—merits punishment, our conscience is, in truth, acting as the voice of God. Paul actually refers to conscience this way in the second chapter of Romans, when he discusses the way the consciences of those who have never been exposed to God's standards have something of the law written on them. Conscience can excuse, but conscience also accuses. The just God will deal with sin as sin deserves.

In the first great doctrinal section of the letter to the Romans (Rom. 1:18–3:20) Paul talks about the ongoing justice of God in his judgment on sin. The certainty in this section is that God is going to judge the world. In addition, God's judgment will be according to truth against all those who do evil. We can expect that sinners will be rejected and condemned for their sins. The background of the good news of the gospel is the bad news about the sinfulness of sin and the certainty of sin's judgment. The first section of Romans and many other places in the New Testament affirm the certainty of that judgment. Indeed, the whole Bible proclaims the certainty of God's judgment.

This must not be regarded as presenting any kind of moral problem as it often is today and has been in the past. On the contrary, we must regard it as the solving of all moral problems. The real moral problem is that God allows sin to run riot in his world. People ask, "Can that be right for God to do?" The Bible answers, "Just wait a moment. God will not allow it forever and sin will one day be judged according to what is deserved."

This is what we must expect from the God of the Bible. He is not a God who keeps his hand hidden forever. One day, he will show his hand by public judgment on all sin as that sin deserves. The day of judgment is unimaginable. Don't try to imagine it because your imagination will simply fail and you will come to the conclusion, "Well, then, it cannot be like the Bible says it is after all." Don't ever be so foolish as to make the measure of your mind the measure of what God can do! God has said what he will do. He will judge all the sin of the human race—past, present, and in whatever future it has, when that day of judgment comes.

God didn't have to choose to save anyone. God didn't have to love sinners after they'd lapsed into sin. But he does have to judge sin because he is that sort of God. This is why the atonement is necessary. The wrath of God, which is against sinners, that judicial resolve to reject sinners for their sin, has somehow to be dealt with. That wrath has to be, to use the technical word, propitiated. In Romans 3:25, the word that in the Greek is *propitiation* is sometimes translated as "sacrifice of atonement." Similarly, John refers to the Lord Jesus as "the propitiation for our sins" (1 John 2:2; 4:10). But translating it as "sacrifice of atonement" doesn't convey what the word actually means. The word *propitiation* in the New Testament expresses the concept of a "wrath absorber," which quenches the judicial wrath of God.

The need for God's wrath to be quenched leads us to our second question. Assuming again that God's purpose is to save sinners, why was the atonement so costly? Why must God send his Son to the shame and agony of the cross? Remember that in order to fulfill his saving purpose towards sinners, God must do justice. God must judge sin. God must be just and manifest his righteous judgment against sin. Paul states this quite explicitly in Romans 3:24–26. Verse 24 explains his reference in verse 21 to the righteousness given by God, which reconciles us to God. This is the gift of righteousness that constitutes our justification, which came freely by God's grace through the redemption that came by Christ Jesus.

As an aside, let me just say a word about that term *grace*. It's a word that existed in secular Greek before the New Testament was written, but in that context, it meant only "gracefulness of conduct." It didn't mean what grace means in the New Testament. Prior to the writing of the New Testament, no one had ever thought the thought that the word *grace* came to express. That thought is what we teach children in Sunday school by using *grace* as an acronym: God's Riches At Christ's Expense. It is the thought of God in mercy giving to the limit in order to bless and save sinners.

Thus we are justified freely by grace through the redemption that came by Christ Jesus, which Paul explains in verse 25. God presented Jesus as a propitiation to quench his wrath. A propitiation effected by his blood and effective for us who are justified through faith. God did this to demonstrate his justice. We see that in the middle of verse 25: "This was to show God's righteousness, because in his divine forbearance he had passed over former sins." Paul is looking back not simply to sins committed during Jesus' lifetime, but to sins committed during the whole Old Testament era. Paul aims to reassure us that God had remitted the sins and forgiven the sinners during the period when sins were atoned for through animal sacrifices according to the Old Testament ritual. But those offerings, though commanded by God and issuing in the forgiveness of sin, couldn't put away the sin of a human being permanently. The basis on which sin was forgiven wasn't clear back then. Thus, there was a puzzle: how was God being just in passing over the sins as he does?

That question is answered as he sets Jesus forth before the whole world, dying in shame as a condemned criminal on a Roman cross. Paul explains that God did this "to show his righteousness at the present time, so that he might be just and the justifier of the one who has faith in Jesus" (Rom. 3:26). The New Testament gospel is of just justification. It's of justified and justifiable justification. Justification is not God shutting his eyes to sin; justification is the fruit of God's dealing with sin through the death of his Son. Jesus endured the true taste of hell for us on Calvary's cross.

The essence of hell is God-forsakenness. The experience of hell was testified to when Jesus said, "My God, my God why have you forsaken me?" Jesus knew perfectly well why he was forsaken, but he asks this question to quote Psalm 22:1. He did this to reveal to his hearers that he was tasting hell for them and let them know that Scripture was being fulfilled. Scriptural prophecy was being fulfilled in what was happening to him and that, surely, is how that word from the cross is to be understood.

God displays his righteousness by judging sin as sin deserves, but the judgment is diverted from the guilty and put on to the shoulders of Jesus Christ, the sinless Son of God acting as wrath absorber. The atonement had to be costly because it was necessary in light of the nature of God, which must inflict retributive punishment on sin. A marvelous wisdom of God consists in his establishing the Lord Jesus as our representative and our substitute because only he could bear and absorb the judgment due to us. Being our representative makes him our substitute, and so he suffers and we go free, just as Isaiah 53 predicted so long ago. God's righteous servant justifies us.

Now you know what Gethsemane was all about. Now you know what the Savior was looking forward to when he sweat great drops of blood (cf. Luke 22:44). Now you see what lay behind Luther's perceptive comment, "Never man fear death like this man." He had to enter into the experience of hell for you and me. He who spared not his own Son but delivered him up for us all has given us perfect certainty and absolute assurance that every good thing will be given to us as well. Nothing he can think to give us now will cost him as much as Calvary. This is the message of our text, and the truth about the necessity of the atonement. This news must be passed on as basic when we proclaim the good news of the gospel.

I would like to conclude with a poem by Joseph Hart, that great Evangelical hymnodist of two centuries ago. I don't call it a hymn because it's an address to men and women, not direct praise to God. But it's also a poem, and it's a poem that crystallizes what's been said and sums it up with wonderful clarity and force. Read it carefully, for this is the true gospel.

> Oh ye sons of men be wise, trust no longer dreams and lies,
> Out of Christ, all mighty power can do nothing but devour.
> God you say is good, that's true.
> But he is pure and holy too, just and jealous is his ire burning,
> with vindictive fire.
> This had all been self-declared: Israel trembled when they
> heard,
> But the proof of proofs indeed is he sent his Son to bleed.
> When the blessed Jesus died God was clearly justified.
> Sin to pardon without blood never in his nature stood.

Worship God, then, in his Son, there his love and there alone.
Think not that he will or may pardon any other way.
See the suffering Son of God panting, groaning, sweating
    blood,
Brethren this had never been had not God detested sin.
Be his mercy therefore sought, in the way himself has taught.
There his clemency is such, we can never trust too much.
He that better knows than we, God himself bid us now to
    Jesus flee.
Humbly take him at his Word and your souls will bless
    the Lord!

2

The Nature of the Atonement: Reconciliation

JOHN R. DE WITT

For our sake he made him to be sin who knew
no sin, so that in him we might become the
righteousness of God. —*2 Corinthians 5:21*

I ATTENDED a pastor's conference some years ago, during which the main speaker made a point that I suppose will be with me for the rest of my life. He said that one should take all the care possible to see that he never ceases to be surprised by Scripture. Given this truth, I do not understand how anyone who loves the gospel—and whose heart is drawn to it—can help but be amazed, even surprised, at Paul's climactic statement in 2 Corinthians 5:21: "For our sake he made him to be sin who knew no sin, so that in him we might become the righteousness of God." This passage looks at the atonement from the perspective of reconciliation and makes a staggering pronouncement that clearly implies our need to be reconciled to God. This text is one that I have studied carefully for many years. Indeed, it is one that I have known virtually all my life, but I recall vividly when it began to impress itself upon me with tremendous power.

I had the privilege to be involved in translating a book on the apostle Paul and his theology from Dutch to English, which spoke extensively on 2 Corinthians 5:21. I had to deal with the Greek, the Dutch, and the English at one and the same time, and in addition to that, with the intent of the author himself. The author saw a profound reality in the words of the apostle Paul, and he expressed himself in a way that was next to impossible to translate into the English language. As I worked, I realized that this manner of expression and the difficulty it produced was a direct result of this passage's capacity to stun the mind when it is deeply considered.

At the outset, we see a legal exchange is in view. Christ, who knew no sin, is legally constituted to be sin by God the Father. That is the essence of the apostle Paul's statement. Christ becomes sin for us sinners, in order that we may become the righteousness of God and may be reckoned the righteousness of God in him. But we must go back before we examine this passage in more detail.

First, our text makes the point that a problem exists between God and us. The biblical teaching on human depravity—that our entire being is permeated by sin—makes the point, with considerable emphasis, that the relationship between God and human beings has been broken. When such a breach has occurred, it will not simply disappear. The Scriptures remind us again and again that God's holiness and justice make it impossible for him to clear the guilty. Think of the words from Isaiah 59:1–2: "Behold, the LORD's hand is not shortened, that it cannot save, or his ear dull, that it cannot hear; but your iniquities have made a separation between you and your God, and your sins have hidden his face from you so that he does not hear." As an illustration, imagine two people who have had a long-standing friendship interrupted by some kind of breach. Perhaps it is reported to one that the other has spoken behind his or her back in a way that is unkind and unfair. It may be that one has traded on that friendship and taken advantage of the relationship. This sort of thing frequently happens, does it not?

This is almost exactly what happened with Donald T. Regan and the late former President, Ronald Reagan. A number of years ago, I read with much interest Donald T. Regan's *For the Record: From Wall Street to Washington*. Mr. Regan was President Reagan's secretary of the treasury and subsequent to that his chief of staff. The two men were not friends; they had no long-term relationship of that kind, yet they still worked closely, successfully, and satisfactorily together until the Iran-Contra affair, after which President Reagan demanded Donald Regan's resignation.

Regan recounts this incident in his book, which is not without its acrimonious side. Indeed, it was in this book that Mrs. Reagan's interest in astrology first came to the public notice. My point is simply that it is the sheerest fancy imaginable that, after the publication of this book, these two men could sit down easily and comfortably with each other, as though nothing had happened and no breach had ruptured their relationship. I am certainly not suggesting that any real parallel can be drawn between such a human breach and the breach that has taken place between God and us, but one can perhaps see a hint of the reality in this example. We cannot be at ease with God and think easily about him with the breach our sin creates. We cannot go to him in prayer, call on him for help, or expect peace with him unless reconciliation takes place. It is important to understand just how deep, wide, and far-reaching is the gulf between God and us.

Second, our text makes it plain that there is need for reconciliation on both sides, for the alienation is not only on our side but on God's side as well. This reminds me of an article that has had some influence in the Reformed and evangelical community. The article was about what Jesus did for us, and it was written by a professor of philosophy at an American university in the Northwest. In his discussion, this learned professor of philosophy challenged what I take to be the biblical teaching on the atonement. Among other things, he said that before we settle upon a theory of Christ's atonement, we should first answer this question: for what purpose, according to the New Testament as a whole, did Jesus Christ die? Was it to change God's attitude towards us or was it to change our attitude towards God? According to this professor, our attitudes, motives, and actions clearly needed changing, while God's did not. This professor even quoted from the passage we are looking at to make his point.

To further his argument he charged both James I. Packer and Louis Berkhof, along with many other prominent commentators, with misconstruing the Pauline argument. Packer argued that if Christ saved us from the wrath of God, then he has quenched that wrath, which would otherwise be directed towards us. Packer thus understood Paul's allusion to propitiation in Romans 3:25. Similarly, Louis Berkhof insisted that Christ's atonement was intended to propitiate God and to reconcile him to the sinner. The professor disagreed, however, and citing Romans 5:10, thought that Paul, for all his talk about the wrath of God, continued to put it the other way around: "While we were enemies, we were reconciled to God by the death of his Son."

This is fascinating because it represents the truth Solomon wrote so many years ago—there is nothing new under the sun. Whether he knew it or not, this professor was arguing precisely what Peter Abelard argued in the twelfth century. Abelard argued that the real effect and influence of the atoning work of Christ on the cross was not towards God but rather towards man. He thought that the whole thrust and purpose of the cross was to move us to an attitude of repentance and love toward God.

This kind of thinking, however, is wrongheaded. The words of Paul in Romans 5:9–11 are sufficiently clear.

> Since, therefore, we have now been justified by his blood, much more shall we be saved by him from the wrath of God. For if while we were enemies we were reconciled to God by the death of his Son, much more, now that we are reconciled, shall we be saved by his life. More than that, we also rejoice in God through our Lord Jesus Christ, through whom we have now received reconciliation.

What Paul means by reconciliation, therefore, is a breaking down of barriers or a restoration of a breached relationship. Thus, he is speaking of a change in attitude not only on the side of human beings, but also on God's side. The Scriptures tell us God must be reconciled just as we must be reconciled.

Third, our text affirms that reconciliation to God is possible. It affirms much more than that, but it seems to me that a necessary and immediate step in our argument is to insist that reconciliation is *possible*. This is crucial because, considering the breach between God and man that the apostle mentions, we would have no hope unless reconciliation was possible. The breach with God is not irreparable; something can be done, and in fact, has been done. Verses 18 and following of chapter 5 show that God has opened himself to us. We begin to see a spark of light, a hint of the coming of the dawn. While at the same time, because of our experience with breached human relationships, it may be difficult for us to understand the assertions made in our text.

I am a pastor and every day I thank God for that privilege. But, as a pastor, I often interact with people whose lives are marked by broken relationships. Whenever I mount the pulpit steps and begin to preach, I think of some of the things that have transpired in that house of worship, where our people gather for praise and to hear the word of God. I have heard story upon story about lives that have been dashed to pieces on the rocks of sin. I recall a particular incident that occurred many years ago, after the service one Sunday morning, when a couple approached me with their children. The man looked as though the weight of the world rested on his shoulders and the woman had tears streaming down her face. She said to me—with her husband standing there, his head hanging down in shame—"What do you do when there is adultery in your family?"

This man had broken faith with his wife. And, as if that were not bad enough, he had communicated to her a disease that he had caught from his mistress. She had every biblical reason for turning her back on him. Yet, she possessed a residual love for him and a desire, under God, to put the marriage back together. Although it is difficult to imagine such a breach being healed, I did see it mended. It was not easy, and not without a great deal of encouragement and a constant need for repentance. Nevertheless, their marriage came to be firm, sound, whole, and healthy, built on a foundation far more solid than anything they had known before! He became a believer in Jesus Christ and she was brought back, after a time of wandering through carelessness and indifference, to faith in the Lord.

No matter how great the ruptures between us are, it is possible for God, in his mercy and grace, to bring people back together. Reconciliation is possible on a human level, but it is also possible on a divine level. Paul is communicating this latter point in 2 Corinthians. Divine reconciliation is possible because the light of the love of God is still burning, even in the darkness of our evil, sin, and rebellion against him. The glorious reality of the gospel is that God has opened himself to us. He has prepared himself to enter a new relationship with us, is willing to receive us, and offers us a place in his own family. We, therefore, can sing with the hymn writer: "Depths of mercy can there be? Mercies still reserved for me? Can my God his wrath forebear, me the chief of sinners bear? I have longed withstood his grace, long provoked him to his face! Would not hearken to his calls, grieved him by a thousand falls."[1] We can all sing that hymn, and yet the door of divine mercy has not been slammed in our faces.

Fourth, from God's side, reconciliation has already taken place. But the statement of our text is stronger than simply reconciliation. Paul says that God literally constituted Christ sin for us. Though he was innocent of any transgressions, Christ was constituted sin so that we might be constituted the righteousness of God in him. A very familiar verse comes to mind when we think of what Paul is saying: "For God so loved the world, that he gave his only Son, that whoever believes in him should not perish but have eternal life" (John 3:16). Many of us memorized this precious verse long ago. It is a part of the basic spiritual vocabulary of every Bible-reading Christian.

1. "Depth of Mercy." Words: Charles Wesley, 1740.

25

And yet it is a verse that contains truths of such staggering magnitude that one may be thought presumptuous even to think about preaching it. I was in the ministry for at least twenty years before I preached on John 3:16. It is deceptively simple. Parts of the verse are plain enough and need little explanation. But other aspects are staggering. God so loved the world that he gave his only begotten Son. God loved the world to such a degree that he was determined to be reconciled to this world, even if it meant giving his only begotten Son. But, in one very important sense, God gave his Son to himself as a propitiatory sacrifice to assuage his divine wrath. This is absolutely astonishing.

Returning to 2 Corinthians, what can Paul mean when he says God constituted his Son sin for us, even though Jesus knew no sin? Such a sentence requires some attention and some study. It is important to underscore that we are not told that the Lord Jesus Christ actually became sinful. Such a suggestion would undercut all biblical teaching on the atonement and the cross. Just as all Old Testament sacrifices had to be without spot and blemish, the great sacrifice of Christ on the cross must be the sacrifice of one who is holy, harmless, undefiled, and separate from sinners. Therefore, Jesus did not become sinful, even though he was like us at all points: "For we do not have a high priest who is unable to sympathize with our weaknesses, but one who in every respect has been tempted as we are, yet without sin" (Heb. 4:15).

Nor is it said in this passage that Christ was made a sin offering for us, despite the fact that he was. Something different from that is being said here that is even more significant, profound, striking, and wonderful than that our Lord was a propitiatory sacrifice. Paul is telling us that God the Father constituted God the Son sin. The Father legally made him liable for the punishment of sin. He consigned his own Son to darkness and separation from his presence. It was as though he, the spotless Lamb of God, were responsible for the sin of the world. Think of it! Clearly this is not in opposition to the Son's own will. In Philippians 2:5–11, Paul tells us that our Lord willingly humbled himself and became obedient unto death, even the death of the cross. But the reality of what the Father did to the Son is no less awesome, even knowing that the Son willingly submitted himself to this plan of redemption. We must understand that the Father stripped the Son of his own holiness and perfection and made him wear the rags of our unholiness and imperfection. He stood in the place of the condemned and the guilty.

This reminds me of something that happened during my student days. My father served a wonderful church on the far south side of Chicago in the 1950s. This church, the First Reformed Church of Roslyn, was doing something then that few other churches were doing in that day. We had a full-time social worker who spent every day of the week in the women's courts. She was a little thing; I don't suppose she was over five feet tall, and there was nothing at all intimidating about her appearance. But she must have had steel in her spine, as well as God's grace in her heart, to do what she did.

When I was in seminary, she invited me and a fellow seminarian to spend the day with her. I think she felt it was time we were stripped of our innocence and given a glimpse of the realities of the world as she knew it. Her name was Grace Willet, and everyone in the courts knew her. She secured a place for us inside the bar, so that we were close enough to the judge, those accused, and their attorneys to hear everything that went on. Most of the women had been arrested the previous night for prostitution or solicitation. One after another appeared and told her unhappy story. It was a sordid day, yet my friend and I learned something about life and saw something we had never seen before. Many people think that ministers are innocent of the realities of the world, which of course is not true. Most pastors listen every day to people's stories and know a lot about sin and the human heart. But one seldom experiences such a concentration of sin and evil as we did that day in the women's courts.

I mention this story to remind us that we must understand what Paul is saying against the backdrop of sin. Sin—the sin of those women in Chicago, the sin of people on the streets of every city in America, the sin of you and me—is what the Father constituted his only begotten Son. God consigned him to a prostitute's place, a murderer's place, an adulterer's place, a homosexual's place, a robber's place, a liar's place, a drunkard's place, a drug dealer's place, and an addict's place. He consigned him to your place and to mine. The Lord Jesus Christ, the son of God who was spotless and about whom from eternity the cherubs sang their ceaseless song, "Holy, Holy, Holy is the Lord God of hosts," is the One who consented to the cross, shame, humiliation, and self-emptying.

Fifth, we must add something more that is of the greatest possible significance. What the Lord Jesus did for us, or rather, what the Father did for us through his Son, is both concrete and particular. The history of Christian thought is replete with attempts to explain the nature of what Christ accomplished on the cross. Some have held that the cross is a powerful attestation that God is the just governor of the universe. Some exhibition of his displeasure with sin was needed, and on that account, he consigned the Son to the cross. Others have said—amongst them Peter Abelard—that the cross is an exhibition of divine love intended solely to move and melt our hearts to the point that we cannot resist responding to the spectacle of the dying Son of God. Such a display prompts us to turn to him in repentance and a loving response of faith with tears streaming down our faces. But the truth is far grander than either of these views, because the Father made the Son to be sin *for* us. That means that forgiveness, reconciliation, and restoration of the breached, ruptured, and broken relationship has not only become possible, but *has become a reality*. The cross means that Jesus Christ took our place, made our sins and guilt his own, and did what needed to be done for those identified with him.

Not too long ago, I read a book by a famous missionary. This man was vastly learned, but he also was able to speak with those who did not share his intellectual giftedness. One day he was talking with a working man named Pete about the very things we have been looking at. After hearing this, Pete responded, "If God should take me to the very mouth of hell and say to me, 'In you go Pete, here is where you belong,' I should say to him, 'True, Lord, I do belong here. But if you make me go to hell, your dear son Jesus Christ must go with me, for he and I are one, and you cannot separate us anymore.'"

That is the reality of what the apostle Paul is speaking about with such grandeur and majesty. Christ took our place—he became sin for us, he submitted himself to consignment for wrath and judgment for us—so that, in him, we might become the righteousness of God. The barriers were broken down. All that stood between us and God was removed and obliterated by Christ's enduring the wrath of his Father on the cross. All of this was so that you and I might be the righteousness of God forever in him. What can we do but sing when we think of truths like these? I think of lovely hymns, which are often sung in connection with passages like this. Perhaps my favorite is "Beneath the

Cross of Jesus."[2] My favorite stanza in that hymn (and one that I hope after pondering Paul's words to the Corinthian church you too can sing) reads,

> Upon that cross of Jesus, mine eye at times can see
> the very dying form of One who suffered there for me;
> And from my stricken heart, with tears two wonders I confess;
> the wonders of redeeming love and my own worthlessness.

2. Words: Elizabeth C. Clephane, 1872. Music: Frederick C. Maker, 1881.

3

The Nature of the Atonement: Propitiation

JAMES M. BOICE

In this is love, not that we have loved God but that
he loved us and sent his Son to be the propitiation
for our sins. —1 John 4:10

THERE ARE MANY WORDS we do not hear mentioned much today in Christian circles. Pastors are reluctant even to use a once-common word like *sin* for fear of offending someone, which in turn could lower the coveted church attendance. Even those pastors who do not give in to this kind of pressure are nonetheless reticent to use "theological jargon," as it is derisively called. There is one word, however, that certainly fits into both categories of common-language terminology and "theological jargon." This word does not occur many times in the New Testament; in fact, only four passages contain it. Some have disregarded it for that reason, which is undoubtedly a mistake. You may not have heard this word, but it is tremendously important for anyone thinking about the cross. The word is *propitiation*.

Despite its infrequent use, this word conveys ideas that are found in both the Old and New Testaments. One reason this particular term is being neglected today is because the concept it expresses is very hard for contemporary people to understand. We generally examine at least three words to explain the nature of the atonement: propitiation, reconciliation, and redemption. With the latter two, it's not as difficult to make associations with contemporary life as it is with the first. When we use the word *reconciliation*, even though we may not use it in the fullest biblical manner, we understand that it has to do with resolving alienation between individuals or various parties. As an example, we speak of mediators who try to reconcile management and labor. We understand what that means and therefore have a basis on which to operate when we talk about reconciliation in the biblical sense.

This is less true of the word *redemption*, but again we have some way of understanding it. It is a commercial term and often has to do with buying. It literally means "buying again." We commonly use this word in relation to something like a pawnshop. We put up an object in order to get some money, and then if we have the money plus the interest, we can redeem the object. In other words, we can get it back out of a kind of bondage. Although that is not a common idea, when we carry it over into the biblical picture, we have a basis for understanding what redemption means.

But none of this is true with regard to the word *propitiation*. Propitiation involves turning aside the wrath of God. However, because it has to do with sacrifice, many modern translations weaken the term, choosing to translate it as a "sacrifice of atonement." This is not all bad, for that is the general idea. But it is a weakening of the term and one of the few unfortunate choices in modern translations. I want to suggest that although the word *propitiation* is difficult and we have to take time to understand it, it is nevertheless of critical importance. Sacrifice and substitution are what the atonement is all about, but we really do not understand the atonement without this idea of propitiation. To understand what the atonement involves, I would like to put this term in a triangular diagram that relates three terms: justification, redemption, and propitiation.

At the top of this triangle, we could write, "God the Father." At the lower left side, we could write, "the Lord Jesus Christ," and at the other corner, on the lower right side, we could write, "us," meaning Christian men and women. The lines connecting those three points stand for the three words I have mentioned: redemption, justification, and propitiation. The line on the bottom stands for redemption, which describes something that the Lord Jesus Christ does in relationship to his people. For example, we can say Christ has redeemed us from the curse of the law. Jesus redeems his people. He sets us free. We do not redeem Jesus; we do not redeem anything. This line expresses that we are the recipients of the action. To make this clear on the diagram, turn the bottom line into an arrow that points to the right, toward us. The line on the right side stands for justification and connects God the Father with us. And just as Jesus redeems us, God the Father justifies us; we do not justify God. This line should be an arrow pointing from God the Father downward, toward us. Finally, the remaining line that connects God the

Father and the Lord Jesus Christ represents propitiation. It is important to understand that this arrow points from the Lord Jesus Christ upward to God the Father because propitiation is something Jesus Christ accomplishes. To put it in grammatical terms, Jesus is the subject of the action and God the Father is the object, therefore, Jesus propitiates the Father.

Even if we do not say anything else in this study of propitiation, we have already learned a great deal from this diagram. We have learned that Jesus Christ is the author and accomplisher of salvation, because two arrows emanate from him. He redeems us, and furthermore, he propitiates the Father. We have also learned something about ourselves—that we do not contribute anything to our salvation. We stand on the receiving side of the triangle; we are redeemed by Jesus and justified by the Father. We do not have anything to offer to this formula. Salvation is by grace and by grace alone, received through the channel of faith, but nevertheless, all of God. God alone is the Savior. We do not save ourselves.

The critical thing to see is that God the Father does one thing on the basis of something else. Based on the work that Jesus Christ accomplished by propitiating (or turning aside) the Father's wrath, God is now free to justify or save his people. God, on this particular formulation, is in the position of a judge who, on the basis of Christ's work, is able to acquit the ungodly. If they stood before him in their own righteousness, the verdict would certainly be in doubt. As soon as we talk about it that way, it is very easy to see why this is of utmost importance.

When we talk about the three terms of the atonement, we do so in the context of ancient culture. Redemption is a commercial term that has to do with buying slaves in the market place. Justification is a legal term that has to do with the judge in the courtroom. Propitiation is a religious term that has to do with sacrifices. In contrast, the theologians of our day often say something like, "We can well understand how the New Testament may have taken over this idea of propitiation, which means to turn aside the wrath of God by means of sacrifice. But if you understand the revelation of God brought by Jesus Christ, then God is a god not of wrath but of love." This argument wants us to do away with the idea of propitiation because, according to these theologians, it is highly inappropriate in the Christian era. Let me further illustrate by quoting one of them.

> Those who hold to the fire and brimstone school of theology revel in ideas such as that Christ was made a sacrifice to appease an angry God, or that the cross was a legal transaction in which an innocent victim was made to pay the penalty for the crimes of others in propitiation of a stern God. This finds no support in Paul. These notions came into Christian theology by way of the legalistic minds of the medieval churchmen and they are not biblical Christianity.[1]

In addition to comments like this, we have also seen an unfortunate change in the way propitiation is translated. The chief culprit in this area is the Cambridge scholar C. H. Dodd, who was very influential in the translation known as the Revised Standard Version. The RSV uses the word *expiation* instead of the word *propitiation* in each of the four texts where the latter can be translated from the Greek. The translators of the RSV were intentionally changing the original idea to emphasize that the problem is not in God but in us. They argue that God is not a god of wrath who must be appeased, but only a god of love. It is merely our own guilt that has to be expiated or lessened, and

---

1. William Neil, *Apostle Extraordinary* (Wallington, U.K.: Religious Education Press, 1963), 89–90.

thus Jesus' sacrifice on the cross was primarily a way to alleviate our guilt and help us to understand that God feels love towards us and not wrath. This is entirely different from the variation in the New International Version, which is used to enhance communication since most people do not know what *propitiation* means. The closest equivalent they found was "sacrifice of atonement," which at least clearly maintains the ideas of atonement and sacrifice. However, it does not do justice to the concept of propitiation.

However, I want to partially defend the theologian I quoted as well as C. H. Dodd. They rightly pointed out that propitiation does not actually mean changing the wrath of God into love for the Christian. This is important because in the ancient world when the worshipper came to present his sacrifice, or propitiate the wrath of God, he thought he was saving himself. He believed that if God was worth anything at all, he must be just, and like a just earthly ruler, has to punish all that is unjust or ungodly. "Now I have done wrong things and I'm well aware of that," the worshipper may have admitted. This is very different from our time, when no one believes they've done anything wrong with respect to God. The ancient worshipper would reason that if the universe really was moral, then the just God would get him sooner or later for what he had done. Therefore, he would have to get God to change his mind in order to be treated nicely. Knowing from common practice that God must be placated with sacrifices, the worshipper would sacrifice to God, perhaps thinking to himself, "I have done something that is a sin—wrongdoing to be sure but not terribly wrong—so I'll bring a little sacrifice. When I have done something very bad, like murdering someone, then I will have to bring a big sacrifice." He offers up his sacrifice and prays that God will be satisfied with it. He hopes God will say, "Well, you did something wrong, but everybody does and it's okay. I see you truly want to make an atonement for your sin, so it will be all right." This is the general idea most ancient people had of propitiation, and from this description it is perfectly evident that this is not a Christian understanding. But, though these ancients were wrong, they were far closer to understanding what is involved in propitiation or salvation than are most people who live in our own time.

Keeping this in mind, there are a couple of things we have to remember about propitiation. First, the wrath of God is real and has to be dealt with. Modern theologians do not want to deal with this and get impatient whenever they come to a text that does. But, of course, it is absolutely impossible to ignore this fact and be true to the text, as is clear in Romans 3:21–25. For the first time in Romans, Paul begins to explain the way of salvation and gives us great words like *justification, redemption,* and *atonement.* Leading up to this point, Paul has been talking about the wrath of God, and it is in this context that Paul begins to speak about propitiation.

Chapters 1 and 2 explain that the wrath of God is displayed against the godlessness and wickedness of men and women because we suppress the truth about him. God has made himself known in nature (not fully, but enough to hold us guilty if we fail to seek him out). We ought to know from nature that we are creatures, and that because we are creatures, there is a Creator. We did not make ourselves or come into being by chance. Rather, there must be a God who made us, and if that is true, we owe him something. Therefore, we ought to seek the true God, worship him, and be thankful to him. But that, of course, is precisely what we do not do. Paul tries to show in the first chapters of Romans that we see the wrath of God in the breakdown of societies, both ancient and modern. The only way this wrath can be dealt with is through the cross of Jesus Christ.

Second, propitiation is never a case of man appeasing God, but rather of God appeasing his own wrath through Jesus Christ. In the ancient system outlined above, the worshipper came with his sacrifice, offered it up, and hoped, perhaps by the size of his sacrifice, to appease the wrath of God. This is not at all the case in Christianity. Although there were sacrifices in the Old Testament, they never took away the wrath of God and never dealt with sin (cf. Heb. 10:4). The Old Testament sacrifices only pointed forward to Jesus Christ and his sacrifice, because only his sacrifice could ever take away sin. This is what we mean when we speak of the necessity of the atonement. Nothing else could take away sin except for the death of the second person of the Trinity, Jesus Christ, the God-man. Propitiation within the Christian scheme is not human beings turning aside the wrath of God. Stunningly, it is God *himself* appeasing *his* wrath. This allows all who are joined to him by saving faith to have the benefits of his atonement. In the true view, wrath is appeased and sin is punished. Nothing is left but the experience and enjoyment of the full love and mercy of almighty God.

Before we move on, we need to note the tendency in Reformed circles to consider sin somewhat mechanically. It's as if God simply does a transaction in the book of heaven that doesn't really concern us. There is truly a transaction, given the terms in which it is presented, but it is never merely mechanical. Romans 3:21–31 puts the emphasis entirely upon righteousness from God that comes by faith, and the word *faith* is used eight times in this passage. Paul is saying that, although propitiation is something that God does, it is not applied to us mechanically but through faith, as God awakens within us that life which is able to turn us from sin to Christ. All of this means that he becomes our Savior and our propitiator.

The second passage where the word *propitiation* is used is Hebrews 2:14–18, and it represents a shift in emphasis. God the Father was emphasized in Romans 3, and now we move to an emphasis on Jesus Christ, the Mediator. Hebrews tells us that Jesus is the merciful and faithful High Priest in service to God, which his atoning death proves. The book of Hebrews is a marvelous study of the person and work of Jesus Christ, which makes its point by contrasting Jesus with things that were known to the Jewish people from their Old Testament heritage. In the first chapter, and on into the second, Jesus is contrasted with the angels and shown to be superior. In the third chapter, Jesus is contrasted with Moses, the great lawgiver, and is again deemed superior. Finally, Jesus is put above the Old Testament high priests and the entire Levitical priesthood. Hebrews repeatedly demonstrates Christ's supremacy in all areas of Jewish life.

Concerning the priesthood of Christ, the author argues that the Old Testament priesthood was inadequate for several reasons. First, the Old Testament priests were themselves sinners. Hebrews 5:3 mentions that they had to make sacrifices for themselves as well as for the sins of the people. The work of the Old Testament priest was inadequate, but it pointed forward to a perfect sacrifice to come. Second, the work of the Old Testament priesthood was incomplete because it had to be repeated over and over again (cf. Heb. 7:27). Third, because Jesus was perfect, the sacrifice was absolutely adequate. Although the blood of sheep and goats did not take away sin, the blood of Jesus Christ, the eternal Son of God, did. This is what all the animal sacrifices pointed to. Finally, the sacrifice was a once-for-all sacrifice. The Old Testament sacrifices had to be repeated day by day, and in the case of the Day of Atonement, year by year. But when Jesus paid the price of our redemption (and our propitiation) by his death on the cross, it ended the sacrificial system.

Hebrews offers an illustration of this through an explanation of what happened on the Day of Atonement, when the high priest went into the Jewish tabernacle, which consisted of two parts. The outer room was called the holy place, and the inner room was called the Holy of Holies or the Most Holy Place. Solomon made a permanent version of this when he built the great temple in Jerusalem. There was an outer court and an inner temple that contained the Holy Place and the Most Holy Place. In the outer court, there were altars for the sacrifices and water for purification. Within the Holy Place stood the seven-branched candlestick and the table of the showbread. A great veil divided this room from the innermost room where the ark of the covenant was housed. This room was the very center of worship.

The ark of the covenant was a wooden box about a yard long and roughly eighteen inches high and eighteen inches deep. It was covered with gold and contained the Ten Commandments, functioning as a receptacle for the law. It also had a covering, and this part of the ark is very important to our present discussion. The Old Testament word for propitiation was based upon the word *cover*, in the sense of "to cover over sin." This covering was called the mercy seat and was made of solid gold. Two figures called cherubim, which had the likenesses of angels, stood at each end of the mercy seat. They faced each other with their wings pointing forward and almost meeting over the top of the ark. God was understood to dwell symbolically in that space between the wings. This is mentioned several times in the Psalms, and is referred to as God dwelling among his people. All of these elements together—the ark, the cherubim, the presence of God, and the law of God—give us a picture of judgment. There is a holy God looking down upon earth and he sees us breaking his law constantly and willfully. We all have broken all of the Ten Commandments.

On the Day of Atonement, the high priest was the only one allowed to enter the Holy of Holies. First, he offered a sacrifice for his own sin and the sins of the people; the former for his own purification. Then he offered a second sacrifice for the sins of the people. He put his hands upon the head of the animal and confessed all the sins of his people, transferring their sin to the substitutionary victim. The victim was then killed, which represented the innocent dying for the guilty. Then the high priest put the blood from the sacrifice into a bowl and passed with it through that great thick veil that separated the Holy Place from the Most Holy Place. He would stand in solemn silence before the ark of God and use a branch of hyssop to sprinkle the blood on the mercy seat. This symbolized propitiation, because it allowed the holy God to look down at his sinful people. Propitiation has occurred and the wrath of God has been poured out against the victim. Now the love and mercy of God are free to go forth and save and bless the sinner. The very heart of Old Testament religion was meant to teach this notion of propitiation.

But notice what happened when the Lord Jesus Christ died upon the cross, as told in the Gospels. The great veil of the temple, separating the Holy Place from the Most Holy Place, was torn in two from top to bottom. This act was God telling us that the perfect propitiation had occurred. Jesus Christ has died, and propitiation has been made. God's wrath is satisfied; it has been absorbed and turned aside. God now stands ready to save and receive any that will come before him in Jesus Christ.

Having dealt with God's work in Romans and Christ's work in Hebrews, we now look at 1 John 4:9–10, where the emphasis shifts to forgiveness, love, and mercy. At the beginning of the letter, John writes about our need for forgiveness and Jesus

Christ as the One in whom we have it. John shows us Jesus as the atoning sacrifice for our sins. When we turn to the fourth chapter, John is writing about the love of God shown to the world because of Christ's sacrifice. The Lord sent his Son as an atoning sacrifice for our sins and this is how we know that he loves us. Elsewhere in Scripture, Luke 18:9–14 probably illustrates this best in the story of the Pharisee and the tax collector. It is justifiably popular because it gets to the heart of what we are talking about—the heart of true religion. Jesus begins this parable with the most extreme contrast imaginable in those times: the highly regarded Pharisee and the hated tax collector. Unfortunately, we have a bad picture of the Pharisees today because of some of the things Jesus said about them. He rightly said they were hypocrites; they were pretending to be righteous when really they were not. He compared them to a tomb that was filled with dead men's bones—it looked nice on the outside but inside it was corrupt (cf. Matt. 23:27). But, let me point out that Jesus' view—correct and flawless precisely because it was the view of the Son of God—was not the popular view of the Pharisees in the ancient world.

The Pharisees were the good people of the day, and there were only about three thousand around at any one time. They were the ones who took the law seriously, unlike the Sadducees (the liberals of the day), who were the political powerbrokers and a kind of posturing religious group. The Pharisees worked very hard at being truly righteous. Putting them into our context, they were like fundamentalists or conservatives. Indeed, they spent a great deal of time finding what the precise meaning of the law was. Paul, himself a Pharisee, wrote his understanding of the popular religion in Philippians 3:4–6 and said that he was "blameless" with regard to the law. The Pharisee in Luke 18 is an upright, moral, godly conservative fundamentalist who goes up to the temple and begins to pray. If he had not prayed, you can be sure that the people would have asked him to. They would have said, "You are the one who should pray. You can lead us in prayer because you know God and are holier than the rest of us." When he prayed, he thanked God that he was not like the robbers, evildoers, adulterers, or even like the tax collector who prayed in the distance. He assumed that because the tax collector was a robber, an evildoer, he was no doubt an adulterer too. Considering that the Pharisee fasted twice a week and gave a tenth of all he got most would agree that he was in the right to pray in this manner. Tithes like his were what kept the temple going, while the sinners didn't give any money.

But then there was the tax collector. He stood off at a distance where he belonged, according to the people. He's not the type of person you would want to have at the front of the church standing on the platform. But this man would not even look up to heaven! He was ashamed of what he was. He could not even face God. While the Pharisee felt he could say, "Hello God! Here I am," the tax collector essentially said, "I am here, this poor man; God have mercy on me as a sinner." This is an amazing contrast that undoubtedly made a strong and clear statement to Christ's hearers. The shocking conclusion in verse 14 might be the most radical thing Jesus ever said: "I tell you, this man went down to his house justified, rather than the other. For everyone who exalts himself will be humbled, but the one who humbles himself will be exalted." Those words would have been unbelievably contrary to popular expectations, leaving people asking, "How could Jesus have said that?"

This statement would have caused people to question the Pharisee and wonder if he was a hypocrite. He had been acting as if he were not a robber, an evildoer, or an adulterer. He was fasting twice a week and giving a tenth of all he received, but maybe he is actually doing all those other things secretly. Maybe he kept double books. Even though he doesn't eat anything unclean in public, maybe he does when he gets home at night. Maybe he sneaks out the back door and goes to the neighbor's house to commit adultery with his neighbor's wife. The people would begin to think that they might have been wrong about the Pharisee. Likewise, they would look at the tax collector in a new way. Even though he is in a bad profession, maybe there are unseen circumstances that change the story. Maybe he was forced into it by poverty. Maybe he really has a heart of gold. All of this points to the fact that we read this story and we *just know* that it can't be true. This simply cannot be what Jesus is teaching. But if it isn't, how then can Jesus say, "I tell you that this man, rather than the other, went home justified before God"?

The answer is propitiation, and that is what this parable is all about. The tax collector's prayer, "God have mercy on me a sinner," is one of the greatest prayers in the Bible. It is so simple—seven words in English and six in Greek. It falls into three parts: an address to God, a praying sinner, and mercy in between. And that phrase "be merciful to me" could quite literally be translated as "make propitiation for me." Even if we took out the first and last part of this prayer, this is significant in and of itself. God is in the center of this combination of ideas that teaches us what true prayer really is. Notice that the Pharisee also began his prayer the same way, with an address to God. But he did not have any consciousness of himself as a sinner and instead thanked God for his righteousness. God is the righteous One, and what Jesus Christ wants us to see is that this Pharisee, though he thought he was praying to God, was not really praying at all.

John Calvin expresses much the same thing in the beginning of his *Institutes of the Christian Religion*. He basically says there that we will never know God without knowing ourselves. We never truly know ourselves without knowing God. We never know God as the Holy One he is until we know that we are the real sinners. Whenever we find ourselves pleading our righteousness before God, we are in trouble. We must come before God recognizing our sin and that God is holy. The tax collector was praying a wise, perceptive, understanding, and spiritual prayer. He prays for God to make propitiation for him. More than merely asking for mercy, he is saying to God, "I come to you on the basis of the mercy seat, on the basis of the blood that was shed in propitiation."

I am not pretending that he understood the fulfillment in Jesus Christ of all that the mercy seat symbolized. The mercy seat, the ark, and the Most Holy Place were all types pointing forward to something that the people of God did not fully understand, because it had not quite come yet. But the tax collector had the right idea. He prayed in essence, "God I have no right to stand before you on my own. I am a sinner, and I deserve to be condemned. The only chance I have is if you will receive me on the basis of the sacrifice of the innocent victim who died in my place to turn your wrath aside." Furthermore, when the tax collector prayed, what he was doing horizontally was exactly what was portrayed on the Day of Atonement, vertically. There was God, dwelling between the wings of the cherubim. There was the law, which we have broken and declares that we are sinners. In between is the mercy seat, upon which blood is shed. That was the way of salvation in the Old Testament times, it was the way of salvation in the day of Jesus Christ, and it is the way of salvation today. There is no other way. If Jesus did not die there would be no salvation for anyone. No other could ever be good enough to bear the price of sin. He only could unlock the gates of heaven. That is the teaching of the Old Testament, the New Testament, and of Jesus Christ.

Let me give one final illustration. William Cowper, a meta-physical poet of the eighteenth century, had a very troubled life. He had a miserable childhood; his mother died when he was only six years old and he was sent off to a boarding school where he was bullied because he was small and weak. He had a fragile mind that gave way on more than one occasion. Twice he tried to commit suicide, and at last, in the year 1756, he was committed to a private lunatic asylum under the care of a man named Dr. Cotton. As was often the case in those days, those deemed lunatics were treated very badly. But Dr. Cotton was a Christian man and he worked very carefully to bring this distraught man out of his depression. He tried to bring Cowper the gospel, which was not an easy task. Cowper was so troubled by his sin that he would cry out in the presence of Dr. Cotton, "My sin! My sin! Oh, for some fountain to open for my cleansing!" But he did not know of any such fountain. Dr. Cotton began to work with him, and by the grace of God, the time came when Cowper found that fountain. Here is the way Cowper told the tale, in is his own words:

> But the happy period which was to shake off my fetters, and afford me a clear opening of the free mercy of God in Christ Jesus, was now arrived. I flung myself into a chair near the window, and seeing a Bible there, ventured once more to apply to it for comfort and instruction. The first verse I saw, was the 25th of the 3rd of Romans: "Whom God hath set forth to be a propitiation through faith in his blood, to declare his righteousness for the remission of sins that are past, through the forbearance of God."
>
> Immediately I received strength to believe it, and the full beams of the Sun of Righteousness shone upon me. I saw the sufficiency of the atonement he had made, my pardon sealed in his blood, and all the fullness and completeness

of his justification. In a moment I believed, and received the gospel.[2]

Cowper had problems later on in his life, but this was a turning point. Out of that experience, he wrote some of our greatest hymns. Indeed, many of them have to do with the atonement.

There is a fountain filled with blood, drawn from Immanuel's
    veins,
and sinners plunged beneath that flood lose all their guilty
    stains.
The dying thief rejoiced to see that fountain in his day,
and there may I, as vile as he, wash all my sins away.
E'er since by faith I saw the stream life flowing wounds
    supply,
redeeming love has been my theme and shall be till I die.

And to that all God's people, who love the atonement with Cowper, can say, "Amen!"

---

2. William Cowper, *Memoir of the Early Life of William Cowper, Esq.* (London: printed for R. Edwards, 1816), 67.

4

The Atonement and the Purpose of God

JOHN R. GERSTNER

*For those whom he foreknew he also predestined to
be conformed to the image of his Son, in order that
he might be the firstborn among many brothers.*
—*Romans 8:29*

THE GREAT DOCTRINES of the Bible are always under
attack, but it seems as though the attacks are increasingly hostile
in our day. Particular objection is made to the doctrines of the
Bible that are considered unique to Calvinism. The objections
take many forms and none of them are really new. However,
there is one doctrine that even the most serious Christians have
trouble with. I am thinking of the doctrine known as limited

49

atonement. To demonstrate the purpose of the atonement in relation to Reformed theology, I will review the basic pattern which is given in terms of the well-known acrostic, TULIP. Although the center of TULIP is our main concern, we will never understand why this doctrine is necessary until we set it in the context of those that surround it.

First, the letter T stands for total depravity. This doctrine simply states that when man first sinned, he died (cf. Gen. 3:17). We need to emphasize at the outset that man is spiritually dead. He's not well, sick, or even terminally ill. He is *dead* in trespasses and sins (cf. Eph. 2:1). His depravity pertaining to all aspects of his personality is total. This is not to be confused with utter depravity, for there is room for "de-provement"! Consequently, the natural man, the slave of sin (cf. John 8:34), exploits every opportunity to sin in every area of his being—in thought, word, and deed, by both commission and omission. Furthermore, even his good works are bad (cf. Gen. 6:5). Total depravity is humanity's one, only, and original contribution to TULIP. The natural man hates God, hates his fellow man, and hates himself. He would kill God if he could, does kill man when he can, and commits spiritual suicide every day. We are the dirty soil in which God plants his flower, and from our filth, produces a thing of divine beauty. Also, as an aside, those who have eyes to see will notice that the TULIP is an infralapsarian plant.

Next, the letter U stands for unconditional election. If man is as depraved as the Bible says he is, then his divine election to salvation would have to be as unconditional as the Bible says it is (cf. Rom. 9:15). How could totally depraved people exercise faith in a God they hate or behave virtuously while averse to virtue? Some have tried to soften this doctrine by referring to "divine foresight." In other words, God looked down the corridors of time and saw who would choose to believe in the Lord Jesus

Christ. Humanity, in this view, still has a step to take, a decision to make. However, if it were merely a matter of foresight in this matter, what would God foresee but sin and unbelief? Therefore, unless he elected to rescue some of the deservedly perishing, none of them would choose God and all would perish. Thus, we see that the election to salvation is absolutely unconditional, but the salvation itself is not. Faith is the prerequisite and good works are the "postrequisite." Faith alone connects us with the salvation offered graciously by God and good works flow from, to borrow the language of the Confession, "a true and lively faith" (WCF 16:2).

The letter L, which will be the focus of our discussion, stands for limited atonement. The atonement of Jesus Christ is the means by which God brings totally depraved, but unconditionally elected, persons to himself without violence to his own inexorable holiness. His mercy constrains him to save, and his holiness restrains him from saving unjustly. God became man in Christ so that he could pay the price of sin and remain God. He did not empty himself of deity when he became incarnate so that the purchase was infinite in value. Thus, the atonement was unlimited in its sufficiency—as in its offer—and limited only in its specific design for those who believe (cf. John 3:16). Those who believe are the elect (cf. Rom. 8:30). The phrase the apostle uses in Romans 9:15—"I will have mercy on whom I have mercy"—at once explains the unconditional character of election and the limitedness of the atonement.

The letter I stands for irresistible grace. The infinitely precious atonement would be of no value without grace being administered *to* the totally depraved persons, who, even though elect, are utterly hostile to God. This had to correspond to what was done *for* them in the atonement. Saving grace needed to not only be provided but also applied. This is by means of union with

Christ and divine regeneration. This divine grace is irresistible or efficacious because it mercifully changes the depraved soul. When a person is born again from above by the Spirit, he then, as a new creature, finds it as natural or as irresistible to come to Christ as, in his depravity, he found it to flee from him (cf. John 3:3–8). Grace is irresistible because it recreates man's will.

Finally, the letter P stands for the perseverance of the saints. The purpose of God would still fail if the last one of Christ's sheep were not brought and kept within his fold (cf. John 17:20–21; 2 Peter 3:9). The saints must persevere and this is only possible and certain if God makes it happen. To borrow an image from the gospel of Luke, God, having put his hand to the plow, never turns back (cf. Phil. 1:6). Because he does not, neither do his saints (cf. Phil.2:11–12). The perseverance by the saints is the consequence of the preservation of the saints. This should encourage us to keep our eyes fixed on Jesus on whom our faith depends from beginning to end (cf. Heb. 12:2).

These brief comments serve as a broad overview of what we mean when we speak of TULIP. These doctrines—in particular total depravity and limited atonement—are under constant assault. To give an example, I remember a little book published around the turn of the last century. It was a direct attack on total depravity—enunciated very clearly and very pessimistically in the Bible—by the man who at that time was probably the greatest living church historian, Adolf Von Harnack. He turned aside from his vast, learned enterprises to write a tiny handbook entitled *The Essence of Christianity*. It was in that book that he coined the expressions "the fatherhood of God," and its concomitant, "the brotherhood of man," both of which became slogans of the liberalism that was so widely popular back then.

The notion that God is a common father of all men and that all men, spiritually as well as naturally, are brothers and sisters was confused with the actual Christian viewpoint. According to the New Testament, as the British scholar Wescott has shown, there's no reference to the common fatherhood of God or the common brotherhood of man. There is no question whatsoever that God is represented as the Creator of all of men and that, as human beings, we are siblings to one another. However, what the New Testament is talking about, in reference to believers, is an adoptive sonship into the family of God, all of whom are reconciled to the Father by his Son, Jesus. Therefore, at the outset of our discussion of the atonement, we must recognize that man is a lost soul. He is under the judgment of God. When Christ talks about the natural man's father, it is not God whom he mentions in this respect (contrary to Von Harnack and others), but says instead these shocking words: "You are of your father the devil" (John 8:44).

As we begin looking at this doctrine of limited atonement, we need also to examine what people have believed about man—who he is and what he's like. Historically speaking, there have been three views concerning this. The first view believes that man is well. This is the liberal view to which we have alluded. The second is a widespread opinion that is far and away the majority viewpoint in contemporary evangelical theology. This is the view that man is not well but neither is he dead. Instead, he is sick, and he is sick unto death. The third and classic view, which we believe is taught clearly in the Scriptures, is that man is actually dead in his sins and totally averse to God. We cannot state it more plainly: everything that man does is abominable. This includes his good works, especially if they pass under the guise of being truly virtuous. Our Lord clarifies this point in Luke 11:13: "You then, who are evil, know how to give good gifts." If man pretends to be virtuous by giving good gifts, he is only adding hypocrisy to his sin.

The Reformed faith has never denied that fallen men and women are endowed with superlative gifts. In fact, the whole tradition is represented by a quote commonly attributed to Augustine (probably the greatest Reformed theologian since the apostle Paul), which refers to the "splendid vices of the heathen." Generally speaking then, God has given talents to those to whom he hasn't given salvation. He has given to us mean folks of the earth, the low and the despised, the choicest of all of his gifts, which we appreciate and from which we benefit. But, because they proceed from an alienated heart, the person who uses these divine gifts does not harshly refer to them as "splendid vices."

We must labor this point because no one will ever be persuaded of election or the atonement unless one has what W. G. T. Shedd called "the most important conviction a person can have," meaning the conviction of sin. I am particularly impressed that most people object to Reformed theology because of the doctrine of the decrees and not because of the doctrine of the atonement. The thing that depresses me most about the objection to unconditional election is that it acts as a red herring. What people really are objecting to is total depravity. It is as if a person comes to a physician complaining of a pain in his shoulder only to be told that there's nothing wrong with his shoulder. He is suffering from gallbladder trouble, but the symptom appears in the shoulder. Most people are like this fictional patient in a spiritual sense. Those who object to the decrees are actually suffering from a lack of conviction of their depravity. Only if you are convinced that you are not just sick, but dead, will you know that there is only one person who can make you alive—the giver of life himself—and therefore be utterly persuaded of the decree of unconditional election. This is where I am so deeply impressed by Martin Luther's *The Bondage of the Will*. Luther was a strong predestinarian, but he came at it both biblically and experientially. One reads his book and realizes that he was persuaded that only almighty God could save him. A realization like this will cure you of any trouble with election.

Once you are persuaded of your own total depravity and satisfied that there must be a divine initiative to account for the life that you have in your soul, you must reflect on this question: when did God decide to cause you to be born again? He did not decide yesterday. He did not have to read the morning paper to find out what you would do. He did not even have to wait on you. God has known all things from the beginning. Whatever he does, he does in accordance with an eternal purpose. This is not just Calvinism; this is theism. Anybody with a rudimentary notion of an eternal, omniscient, infinite Being, knows that what this Being has ever intended to do, he has always done. Election comes right out of this understanding. Once a man is persuaded that his life came from God, he must acknowledge that God must have made up his mind to bestow life upon him from all eternity. That is unconditional election. I know this experientially just as Martin Luther knew it experientially. There is nothing in John Gerstner and there is nothing in you that would ever account for our turning to God. I know that if God saw fit in his consummate grace to condescend to my low estate, he did so with an eternal purpose.

Some believe that Scripture contradicts this doctrine and support this position with Romans 8:28–30.

> And we know that for those who love God all things work together for good, for those who are called according to his purpose. For those whom he foreknew he also predestined to be conformed to the image of his Son, in order that he might be the firstborn among many brothers. And those whom he

predestined he also called, and those whom he called he also justified, and those whom he justified he also glorified.

At first glance, this text of Holy Scripture certainly suggests that election is anything but unconditional. It even appears that God is looking down the ages and foreknows that a man is going to turn to Christ. Then, because he foreknows that a man will indeed exercise faith, he predestines him, calls him, justifies him, and glorifies him. From this perspective we stand where the broad evangelical spectrum of the church puts itself, and we look at this text, for the moment, as an Arminian does. According to this interpretation, this text says, "Whom God foreknew would believe, them he did predestine, and whom he predestined, them he called, and whom he called, them he justified."

This text is commonly called the golden chain of salvation, but the Arminian interpretation presents a built-in problem. Although many others were implied, there are only five links mentioned: first foreknowledge, then predestination, then calling, then justification, and then glorification. But, looking at the links of calling and justification, another vital aspect emerges. To what are we called but to faith? By what are we justified, but by faith? In other words, though faith is not specifically listed as one of these links in the golden chain, it is unmistakable and inescapable. The calling here described is the call to come unto Jesus, to believe in Jesus, and to trust in Jesus. Furthermore, the heart of the gospel is justification *by faith* alone. When we are called to faith and then exercise that faith, we are justified.

Just in case all this is not obvious, let us be reminded that the Arminian view teaches that *foreknew* here means, "whom God foreknew as *believing*." This view states that *foreknow* means "foreknow as believing," which would imply that whom God foreknew as believing, he predestined to believe, and whom God foreknew would have faith, he predestined should have faith. Remember that faith is to what we are called and by which we are justified. Therefore, is it not absurd to say that God foreknows that we will believe something and then he predestines us to believe it? Based on this understanding, the Arminian view is utterly untenable and impossible. It represents God as knowing we'll do something and then predestining us to do it, which does not make any sense at all.

Some may object that we have our own problem at this point because we admitted at the outset that the word *foreknow* suggests primarily the idea of having knowledge before the beginning of time. We do not handle this problem the way our evangelical majority does because their interpretation is out of the question. Their view is impossible, does violence to the Word of God, and won't let the Word of God have the final say. So what does Romans 8:28–30 teach?

Before we go any further, we have to address that we are working with a bad translation due to limitations of the English language. There is only one English word to explain the idea of knowing or foreknowing. The word *know* means both "information about" and "an encounter or experience with someone or something." This was how William James tried to break it down. Here's one definition that contains both concepts: "an acquaintance with or a knowledge about something." It is interesting that almost every other existing language has two words for these ideas. But the English language has only one, and consequently that one word *know* could be taken either way, given our above definition. It could mean, "merely have information about," so that in the context of Romans 8:28–30 it would mean, "foreknow that God had information about him from all eternity." Alternatively, it could also mean, "foreknow" in the sense of fore own, fore appropriate, or fore love. In this particular passage, it won't make any sense just to say, "whom he knew beforehand" in the sense of having information about beforehand. Therefore, it must be the latter meaning. With this translation the passage would read: "Whom he fore loved and fore owned, them he predestined to be conformed to the image of his Son."

Some may wonder why translators don't translate it this way. Most likely it is because the Greek word *proginosko* is literally translated as "know." Recall our previous statement that we are up against the limitations of the English language, and people just don't want to take this kind of liberty. Personally, if I were to run a translation committee, I would have problems with translating it other than "know." But the Bible is full of uses of the word *know* in the way I have suggested. When Psalm 1:6 says, "For the LORD knows the way of the righteous, but the way of the wicked shall perish," surely it does not mean that God is simply familiar with the way of the righteous and not with the way of the wicked. He knows the way of the righteous, and he loves the way of the righteous. When Christ will say to some in the last day, "I never knew you; depart from me" (Matt. 7:23), he is not pleading ignorance. He means, "I have never been in communion with you, I have never owned you, and you have never owned me." This is a very common use of *know*, although I have never tabulated it. But if you did count up the occurrences of the words *know* and *foreknow* in the Bible, I believe they would be much more commonly used in the sense of intimacy. Therefore, Romans 8:28–30 can be understood to mean, "Whom God fore loved, them he predestinated to be called and justified and glorified." Paul is teaching that because God loved those whom he chose, he provided the atonement for them.

The purpose of the atonement, therefore, is to carry out the fore-loving purpose of a merciful God for totally depraved men and women. I tucked in a little phrase here about the fact that though this is an unconditional love on God's part, it is a choosing of us—an utterly noxious, repulsive, and totally sinful people. There is nothing for God to grab hold of. He holds his nose and he stops his ears when he chooses us. We are utterly detestable, and yet while we were dead in trespasses and sins, God loved us and Christ died for us. In this sense of the word *unconditional*, it is indeed utterly unconditional; we do not have anything to do with it. We do not have anything that recommends us to God. But never misunderstand that God's fore loving and his unconditional election are free of conditions. As I said before, faith is a prerequisite and good works are a "postrequisite."

I recall giving a talk at Seattle Pacific College some years ago in an open colloquium with the students present. One student said to me out of thin air (I do not know what his purpose was), "Dr. Gerstner, you're a Calvinist." So I replied, "Yes," and that was the end of that. We went on with other questions and about a half an hour later the same fellow raised his hand and said, "Since you believe it's perfectly all right to sin, may I go and do whatever I please?" Being a Calvinist meant to this young man that I thought as long as a person was unconditionally elected he could sin as he pleased. I disabused him of that particular notion and I would disabuse anyone else of the same notion. Rather, let me say that the unconditional choice of God produces in us a path of holiness and a way of living that is truly virtuous, though far from perfection.

Returning to our main point, limited atonement comes right out of the purpose of the God who fore loved a multitude, which no man can number. We must be clear that God was not pleased to fore own everyone. But because in his mercy he did own some, and because he is an infinitely holy God, he must bring them into his presence by a way that purifies, justifies, and sanctifies them, while satisfying his holiness. That is what the atonement really does.

Again, I think of an experience I had that is very common these days. Some people, in evangelical fervor no doubt, feel much more comfortable about the idea of the atonement then they do with election. I recall a time when I was preaching in the Boston area a series of sermons on Romans on two consecutive Sundays. After the second Sunday morning service, we had a question period and around seventy-five people stayed for it. Because I had preached in the morning service on Romans 8:28–30, the very first question was, "Dr. Gerstner, why do you say so much about predestination? Why don't you say more about the atonement?" I reminded the questioner that I had already preached eight sermons, which showed the need of the atonement, the nature of the atonement, and the application of the atonement. My sermon that morning had been the first reference to the decrees and that was because it was inescapably there in Romans 8. I went on to explain that if there were no election, there would be no atonement. If God had not fore loved and unconditionally chosen us, he would never have sent his Son into the world to redeem us from our sin. It is utterly impossible to extol the atonement too much, but the fact remains there would be no atonement without election—if God had not unconditionally elected his people to eternal salvation. In terms of TULIP, the very root of the flower is the elective purpose of God that is planted in us, the dirty soil. You might call the atonement the stem, which develops out of the root and leads to fruition from it. But if there had been no root that stem would never have developed and that flower would never have come into being. Thus, the atonement is the actual carrying out of the elective purpose of God. When we sing that "all the light of sacred story, gathers 'round its head sublime,"[1] we ought to remember there would be no head sublime and there would be no cross in which we glory, if there had not been this redemptive purpose of God.

Whenever we are thinking about the atonement and the purpose of God, it is only natural to mention the first great book on the subject written by Anselm in the eleventh century, *Cur Deus Homo*. Translated, this title is a question: Why did God become man? This is the first classic articulation of what I have been explaining: totally depraved sinners, who had violated the honor and glory of God and had committed an infinite fault, could only hope for one way by which the honor and dignity of God could be restored—an infinite sacrifice. To provide this sacrifice, God had to become man and endure the punishment that would repair the damaged honor of God. So God became man in order to suffer, and his suffering was of infinite value because it was God who became man. That is the thrust of *Cur Deus Homo*.

In relation to Anselm, I always remember the time that I had the privilege of being a student of the late John Murray. In his lectures, he was fond of saying that the atonement is "antecedently, absolutely necessary." What he meant by that very precise language was that the atonement was neither consequently nor relatively necessary. Even the great Thomas Aquinas, who believed in the atonement and because of its factuality insisted upon it, unfortunately felt that it was not antecedently necessary. He believed that God might have saved men some other way than by becoming incarnate and providing the atonement. However, since God did not choose another way, the atonement becomes absolutely obligatory,

1. "In the Cross of Christ I Glory." Words: John Bowring, 1825. Music: Ithamar D. Conkey, 1849.

although only *consequently* in this view. To the contrary, Murray said that the atonement must be antecedently, absolutely necessary, for there was no other way it could have been done. Murray could not conceive of God sending his only Son into this world to die on a hideous cross for the redemption of people if it were not necessary. It had to be and it was absolutely necessary that he should take our nature upon himself. In that nature, the Lord Jesus Christ made a truly, infinitely, and satisfactory expiation of our guilt in the atonement in which we glory.

Though it may surprise some, the proof that Christ accomplished this for his elect people is found in John 3:16: "For God so loved the world, that he gave his only Son, that whoever believes in him should not perish but have eternal life." This verse is constantly focused on limited atonement and gives it a classic exposition. If it were opposed to the idea of the limited or specific atonement, it would make no sense whatsoever. This text gives us another example of what happened in our earlier examination of Romans 8:28–30. At first glance, it looked as if Romans 8:28–30 were against the idea of unconditional election. But, with only the slightest reflection, we found a classic affirmation of the very doctrine in question. The same goes for John 3:16, which, at first glance, seems to teach that Jesus Christ died for all people. But if we look at it carefully, we see an obvious problem.

All evangelicals believe that universal salvation is a heresy. Believers do not constitute the totality of mankind. We know this because John 3:16 clearly says that God loved the world and gave his only Son for each *believing* individual. A believing individual is a person whom God has fore loved from all eternity and predestined to call and justify by faith. This faith, which is the gift of God and the product of the new birth, is also the sovereign work of the Holy Spirit in us. With this understanding, we might translate John 3:16 this way: "God so loved the world that he gave his only Son, that the elect in all the world should not perish but have everlasting life." Just a moment's reflection on the text confronts a person with the realization that this is a classic passage on limited atonement. Indeed, John 3:16 is the choicest passage for this particular doctrine.

I must draw our discussion to a conclusion with a reminder— Christ's great atonement for his people would have failed if he hadn't done *in* us what he had done *for* us on the cross. This again follows automatically from our total depravity, which requires God to take an initiative of a most radical sort. No amount of pleading, threatening, and praying is going to change a person who loves the darkness and hates the light. He has to be born from above, and this is what we mean by irresistible grace. God has to change the sinner's heart, but he does not force the will. It is true that the word *irresistible* can suggest the idea that someone is dragged, kicking and protesting, into the kingdom by a power greater than he. In one sense, this is accurate because the natural man just wants to revel in the world, the flesh, and the devil. He wants to go his sinful way, and he hates religion and everything about it.

Some people think the Reformed define irresistible grace in this way. In other words, they think that we believe the Almighty drags the sinner to heaven even though he wants to live a hellish life. But here's an example to illustrate the absurdity of this view. Imagine a man named Joe Saint. He very much wants to be a holy person. From his infancy, he has been interested in religion. He wants to cultivate morality. Imagine a scenario where his name is not written in the Book of Life and the angel says, "I'm sorry, Joe. You are a nice guy and all the rest of it, but your name is not written here. I have looked and there is no Joseph Saint. So, I'm sorry, Joe, you just have to go the opposite way." So he goes screaming into hell in spite of his love for heaven, while some other guy—with no desire for heaven or Christ or anything Christian—passes him, being dragged reluctantly into glory. Although this sounds insane, I could show you serious theological documents that conceive of the Reformed faith teaching something this absurd. God does not do this, and God cannot do it. God can't force the will. The will is a person choosing. If I am making a choice and God forces me to choose something other than I will, then it is not my choice. This kind of objection to Reformed theology—that a person who wants to go to heaven cannot—is in the same category with squaring a circle. If God squares a circle, it just is not a circle anymore. If God forces my choice, it is simply not my choice.

Irresistible grace means that God gives us a new nature so that what we previously hated, we now love and cannot keep away from it. It is irresistible in the sense that it becomes natural. It is efficacious in the sense that it becomes your very disposition. A man becomes a man of violence for heaven, as the Puritans used to say. You will not be put off from obtaining this blessed possession. Previously you hid your face from God, you turned away from him, and you would have nothing to do with the Holy One of Israel. But now that you are a new creature—now that you have been born from above—you hate the darkness you once loved, and you love the light that you hated. You just cannot be kept out of the kingdom. Grace is irresistible in this sense of the word.

In closing, let us notice that, even on this presentation, everything could potentially be lost. Even if God elected from all eternity a people to be saved, sent his Son in the fullness of time, and made them over again by his great creative Spirit, if God ever let go and ceased to work in us, we would lapse immediately into the sin from which we had been delivered. Unless he preserves us, we will never realize the fruit of the atonement that was made for us.

I have a friend whom I run into about every five years. He does not believe in the perseverance of the saints. In fact, I do not know anybody who disbelieves in the perseverance of the saints more vigorously than this friend. But, my, does he have assurance! He is full of confidence that he will be with God forever. I ask him, "If there is no biblical doctrine that the saints would certainly persevere and that God will preserve them, how can you be so sure that you are going to arrive at the pearly gates?" He has no answer for this question, so I usually say to him that he is operating with stolen capital. He is secretly slipping in my doctrine and enjoying the fruits of the perseverance of the saints, while his doctrine absolutely rules out such assurance. I like to remind him that it is not honest for a Christian to steal somebody else's doctrine and enjoy the truth which one denies. But nothing seems to bother him, and he goes on enjoying an absolute confidence. Indeed, he seems even more confident than I am! The difference is that I have a reason to be confident, and he does not.

If you are going to throw your hat in the air and rejoice to the finished work of Jesus Christ on the cross, it is because he is going to continue to work in you "to will and to work for his good pleasure" (Phil. 2:13). God works in you, and you work out. Our tendency is to think that since God is going to work in us, we can relax. God has the situation under control. On the other hand, given the previous verse ("work out your own salvation") our reasoning could be that we have to work it out because God is not doing it. Both of these options are wrong. But here is what we should think along with the apostle Paul—I will work out precisely because God is working in me. God is preserving his elect, therefore they will persevere and they can rejoice now. Heaven is as good as theirs. When Jesus Christ sees them on the way—redeemed from their sins, translated out of the kingdom of darkness, established in holiness—no one will ever be taken out of his hand. That is when the Lord Jesus Christ will see the fruit of his atonement. He will see his seed, all of God's elect, and he will be satisfied. Praise his name!

5

Sacrifice and Satisfaction

R.C. SPROUL

Christ redeemed us from the curse of the law
by becoming a curse for us—for it is written,
"Cursed is everyone who is hanged on a tree."
—*Galatians 3:13*

ANYONE WHO HAS ever attended seminary can recall a certain number of unforgettable experiences. In my case, the thing that comes to mind is something that happened in a preaching class I had years ago, the format of which was somewhat intimidating. A student would be given the assignment to prepare a sermon on a given text. After he was done preaching, the students and the professors were given time to critique the content and style of delivery. One of my classmates preached what I thought was a brilliant and stirring sermon on the cross of Christ, in which he stressed one aspect of the suffering of Christ. His sermon described what was involved in Jesus' being a substitute for us, thus satisfying the demands of God's justice and wrath. Normally, at the conclusion of a sermon the professor would open the floor and let the other students respond. But on this particular occasion, the professor was so incensed by the sermon that, instead of turning it over to the class, he offered the initial critique. The critique came by way of a question that was meant to be rhetorical, to say the least. The professor asked, "How can you possibly preach a sermon on the substitutionary and satisfaction view of the atonement in this day and age?"

When that sort of thing happened in seminary, I tried very much to behave myself. My strategy was to take the role of discretion and diplomacy rather than antagonism. But in this instance, I must admit that I was angered by the professor's question. I jumped to my feet and said in a way that I am sure was inappropriate, "How can *you* challenge this man's prerogative to preach the substitutionary, satisfaction view of the atonement in this day and age?" We could ask a similar question today. What is it about modern culture and theology that has made the cross of Jesus Christ obsolete or antiquated? Why would anyone not want the sinner to have at his disposal a sacrifice that satisfies the demands of God's wrath?

I pointed out to the professor that, at that time in the history of theological education, the accent was still on the teaching of Dr. Karl Barth, the famous neo-orthodox theologian. He was the hero of the hour and most of the courses focused our attention on his work. I told the professor that even Dr. Barth (who was by no means an evangelical) believed that the most important word found in the New Testament is the Greek word *huper*, which in English can be translated "in behalf of." Dr.

Barth thought this little word was so important because it was used again and again to focus on the fact that what Jesus Christ did on the cross, he did not do for himself. Nor did he do it as an example to be emulated by those who observed his activity. The work that he performed was a work done *huper*—for other people, in behalf of them, and as a substitute for them. He laid down his life *for* his sheep.

But what about that word "satisfaction?" This is what causes us to shrink back because it puts us on a collision course with our modern notions of grace and mercy. It reminds me of a little experiment I tried in a Reformed church in western Pennsylvania. We were setting up examinations for students coming under care, similar to a modern day committee of candidates and credentials. Part of my task was to help prepare the questions of examination for those coming for ordination. One section of the test was a true or false section, the bane of every close thinking scholar and student! The statement that I invented, to the embarrassment of the rest of the committee (and most of the presbytery), was, "True or false: It is in the cross of Jesus Christ that we find the only means by which God clears the guilty." I tried it on the men who were already ordained to see if it was a fair question for the students coming up for ordination. Every one of these astute and totally committed Reformed pastors indicated that the statement was true.

It was a trick question, I must admit. Essentially, I wanted to know if the men coming under care had ever thought about this: how many ways are there that God clears the guilty? My friends, there are no ways by which God clears the guilty! The question is manifestly false, particularly if you have ever read and paid close attention to the Westminster Confession of Faith. It tells us explicitly that God never clears the guilty.

God *redeems* the guilty. He pays the price for the reconciliation of the guilty. But he never exonerates, clears, or acquits those he says are guilty by reason of their sin. The guilt of sinners is clearly set forth in the Bible—the indictment is there—and that is why there is an atonement. Guilt demands satisfaction. Somehow, the professor in my seminary class thought that this kind of thing was beneath the dignity of God. He could not fathom that God should require that his holiness be maintained, or that his justice be honored. He had confused mercy and justice.

What I would like to do in this chapter is not simply rehearse for you, in abstract theological terms, the essence of the historic position concerning the atonement—sacrifice and satisfaction. Rather, I would like to turn your attention to a historical and biblical representation of the drama of what actually happens in the atonement, using the Hebrew thought forms and patterns that we find within the Scriptures. In other words, I want to look at just one aspect of the sense in which Christ's offering on the cross is seen both as a sacrifice and as an act of satisfaction.

Let us examine a passage that is often overlooked in our consideration and discussion of the cross. I have found it to be one of the most poignant and dramatic statements in the New Testament about the nature of the cross. I am referring to the third chapter of Paul's epistle to the Galatians. We also see here Paul's rehearsal of the classic doctrine of the Reformation, justification by faith alone.

> For all who rely on works of the law are under a curse; for it is written, "Cursed be everyone who does not abide by all things written in the Book of the Law, and do them." Now it is evident that no one is justified before God by

the law, for "The righteous shall live by faith." But the law is not of faith, rather "The one who does them shall live by them." Christ redeemed us from the curse of the law [pay attention to this] by becoming a curse *for* us—for it is written, "Cursed is everyone who is hanged on a tree"—so that in Christ Jesus the blessing of Abraham might come to the Gentiles, so that we might receive the promised Spirit through faith. (Gal. 3:10–14)

In this passage, Paul pits the concepts of blessing and curse against each other, creating an antithetical relationship. He uses this curse motif to call attention to what Jesus did for us on the cross. Paraphrasing Deuteronomy 21:23 as, "Cursed is everyone who is hanged on a tree," Paul says that Jesus has redeemed us from the curse by becoming a curse for us on the cross. Jesus Christ is cursed by God Almighty. What does that mean?

This language is not part of our popular theological vocabulary. What does the Bible mean when it speaks of blessing and curse, particularly the term *curse*? When we hear this word today, what does it conjure up in our minds? Perhaps you think of some witch doctor or some voodoo practitioner who uses a little replica doll and pins and needles to put a curse upon unknowing victims. Or, maybe you recall the sinister old movie character Oilcan Harry, who goes off into the sunset twitching his mustache and saying, "Curses! Foiled again!" My point is simply that the word is archaic. We hardly ever use it in our vocabulary, but it is a word that is used repeatedly in the Bible. Furthermore, it is the word that comes from the pen of the apostle as he focuses his attention on the essence of what happens in the cross of Christ. This is because Paul is thinking of the cross in Old Testament terms.

In covenant terms, Paul cites Abraham in this passage as the father of the faithful. He speaks of the blessing motif, as well as the cursing motif, which calls our attention back to the Old Testament and to the law. We read, for example, in the section of the Old Testament that Paul is quoting from, "See, I am setting before you today a blessing and a curse" (Deut. 11:26). Basically, God goes on to say, "If you keep my covenant to which you are sworn by the sign and seal of circumcision then you will receive blessing. But if you disobey my law then I will curse you." Then follows a litany of both blessings and curses that are spelled out for us throughout Deuteronomy and then again in chapter twenty-eight, verse fifteen, which reads, "But if you will not obey the voice of the LORD your God or be careful to do all his commandments and his statutes that I command you today, then all these curses shall come upon you and overtake you." Pay attention to these verses that follow. They're really grim. This is not gospel. This is bad news.

> Cursed shall you be in the city, and cursed shall you be in the field. Cursed shall be your basket and your kneading bowl. Cursed shall be the fruit of your womb and the fruit of your ground, the increase of your herds and the young of your flock. Cursed shall you be when you come in, and cursed shall you be when you go out. The LORD will send on you curses, confusion, and frustration in all that you undertake to do, until you are destroyed and perish quickly on account of the evil of your deeds, because you have forsaken me. (Deut. 28:16–20)

Did you catch all of that? Cursed when you stand up. Cursed when you sit down. Cursed when you go to the city. Cursed when you go out of the country. Cursed be your wives. Cursed be your fields. Cursed be your business. Cursed be your family relationships. Cursed be your descendants. Cursed be your generations. Cursed be every aspect of your life. God is saying to them that life will be one huge, monumental curse.

I think it behooves us to understand what a curse is from a biblical perspective. If the kind of threatening we just saw hangs over our heads like the sword of Damocles, what does it mean to be cursed by God? We can look at that question two ways. We can look at it by way of contrast with the concept of blessing, and we can look at it directly.

To understand what the curse is, we must first understand what it is not. The curse is contrasted with the blessing. If we understand what the blessing is—what it means to be blessed in biblical categories—it will help us understand the opposite of blessing, which is cursing. My favorite way of illustrating the meaning of blessedness biblically is to call attention to the classic Hebrew benediction. You are probably familiar with it but let us look at it for a moment anyway. "The Lord bless you and keep you; the Lord make his face to shine upon you and be gracious to you; the Lord lift up his countenance upon you and give you peace" (Num. 6:24–26). You've heard this, if you are a churchgoer, probably hundreds, if not thousands of times. But you may wonder what it means, and why it emerged as the central form of benediction in the Hebrew community.

Remember that the nicest, kindest, and most loving thing that one Jew could ever say to another was, "The Lord bless you and keep you." This part of the benediction has two distinct elements in it: blessing and keeping. This concept of keeping would have meant something to a Jew who lived the life of a pilgrim. The Jews lived a semi-nomadic existence—always packing their bags, no permanency, looking for a country, looking for a city whose builder and maker is

God—that was their route. Stability and permanence were foreign to the Jew, and to some extent, still are to this day. The wandering Jew is caught up in the drama of the quest for stability and permanence. According to the Old Testament, the Jew wants to experience what it means to be kept.

This is what is meant by the concept of keeping, but I still have not said anything about the concept of blessing. Moses uses a literary device here called parallelism, which basically means that if you do not understand something in one stanza, look at the other stanzas to shed light on it. What does the second stanza say in this instance? "The LORD make his face to shine upon you and be gracious to you." What about the third stanza? "The LORD lift up his countenance upon you and give you peace." How does the Jew understand what it means to be blessed? According to this, to be supremely blessed of God is to be able to look at him face to face. Blessing is when the Lord makes his face shine upon you and lifts up the light of his countenance upon you. The Jew is saying, "That's my wish for you, my brother Israelite. That's my benediction. This is the good saying that I have for you—that somehow, someday you will experience a face to face encounter with God."

The Jewish nation has experienced all kinds of glorious benefits at the hands of God, for they were uniquely chosen by him. From the blessing of the patriarchs, to the promise of redemption, to being called out of the world to be God's people, the Jews have been a blessed people. But above all this was the desire to see God. We need to see why, scripturally, this matter of seeing God was such a big deal.

Remember that Adam and Eve were expelled from the garden, and God put an angel with a flaming sword there so that no man could see the face of God. This was because

God's eyes are too holy as to even look upon iniquity (cf. Hab. 1:13). The Scriptures tell us again and again that no man shall ever see God and live. So, for the Jew, blessedness was a proximate matter. They described and measured blessedness in quantitative terms, in terms of how close they could approach the living God. When Moses came down from the mountain after seeing the back of Yahweh his face shone with such effulgent glory and radiance that the people could not bear to look at their leader; they had to ask him to veil his face! All Moses was doing was mirroring and reflecting the radiance of the back of God.

Blessedness for the Jew meant coming always closer to the presence of God. Remember that God had said that he was in the midst of the people. God is near. God is present, and to be in the presence of God for the Jew is the ultimate experience of blessedness, or at least the penultimate experience of blessedness. The ultimate experience, of course, is in heaven where we will be so close to God that the ultimate prohibition is removed and we can gaze into his face with no veils and no barriers. This is the supreme eschatological hope of the Christian that we hear so rarely about today from the pulpits in our land. It is what the theologians call the *visio Dei*, the beatific vision, when our eyes will behold the living God. Think of 1 John 3:2, which contains that unspeakable and ineffable promise. John tells us that the astonishing matter of love is that we should be called the children of God. Let me paraphrase what John says there: "But we are called the children of God, and we do not know yet what we shall be like, but this much we know: when he comes we shall be like him because we will see him as he is in himself."

75

Even in our redeemed state of justification, though we are cloaked with the righteousness of Christ already, we are not yet glorified and purified, and the promise of the beatific vision throughout Scripture is given only to one class of people—those who are altogether pure are the ones who are promised the benediction of Jesus. These are the ones who receive the promise of the beatitude, "Blessed are the pure in heart, for they shall see God" (Matt. 5:8).

Returning to our passage in Numbers, this was the great wish of the Jew for his brother. He would have said, "May you see the living God someday face to face and experience the ultimate state of blessedness that any creature is capable of." Would this not satisfy your soul forever? One glimpse, one second to look into the face of God—it would be the end of theology! No more theology lessons and sermons, it would be all over. Just to see him once and then words would become hopelessly inadequate. That would be the meaning of one Jew saying this to another.

The curse is the opposite of all this. The curse is not merely to have the veil come down over the radiance of the face of God. It means more than that. Not only is God's face obscured in the curse, but God also turns his back in the act of cursing. After God turns his back, he departs from us, and he leaves us isolated from his presence with no benefits of his presence and nothing to enjoy. How many times have you heard statements like, "War is hell"? Or maybe you've heard someone say, "Well, I sure went through hell in that experience." And how many times have you heard it said of hell, "Hell is not a lake of fire. It's just separation from God"? I have heard students say these kinds of things. For my part, I would rather have the lake of fire. Does that surprise you?

We need to be careful. There is unspeakable misery in this world—pain, sorrow, and grief beyond comprehension—but there is no corner of this earth today where you will find the total absence of the presence of God. There really is no experience so miserable, painful, or grievous in this world as this absence would be. There is no place in this world where God's common grace does not reach. We can never compare separation from God with anything in this life. Any horror of this world is really nothing compared to the horror of hell, where there is absolutely no penetration of the blessing of God. What does the term *curse* mean in the Bible? Darkness, outer darkness, where there is only weeping and gnashing of teeth. The curse is when we are, as circumcision so eloquently signifies, *cut off* from all benefits of the presence of God.

But the Old Testament also speaks of atonement. The Old Testament day that foreshadows and prefigures the event of the cross perhaps most particularly is the Day of Atonement. In the Hebrew language, it is known as *Yom Kippur*. On this day, two animals were sacrificed. The first was a lamb without blemish. This lamb was offered as propitiation, as a sacrifice on the altar. It was killed, destroyed, burned, and consumed. The second animal was the scapegoat. The priest ceremonially would go and lay his hands upon the scapegoat. Symbolically, the priest was transferring the sin of the people on to the back of the scapegoat. The significant thing is what is done with the scapegoat. It wasn't killed but, from the Jewish perspective, it met a fate far worse than death. It was driven into the wilderness outside the camp. It was banished and exiled from the locus of the presence of God.

All of this drama is there, unfolded in the passion of our Lord. I must confess that if I ever again hear a minister stand up on

Good Friday and give a graphic description of the unspeakable grotesque nature of the cross, I think I might just lose it. I want to ask such ministers, "So what?" Thousands upon thousands of people have died by being nailed to a tree. Many men have gone through much more excruciating pain than did Jesus of Nazareth. But here is the point that many such overly graphic illustrations miss: only Jesus, in the midst of his death, suffered the fullness of the unspeakable horror of the unmitigated curse of God in his death. So horrible was this aspect of his death that I doubt if Jesus was even aware of the nails. The significance of his mode of death is that it was Roman. It was a pagan execution and that indicated that he was an alien to the commonwealth of Israel.

Jesus lived out the drama of the curse. The first thing that happened to him, that the Scriptures might be fulfilled, is that he was delivered to the Gentiles for judgment. He came to his own city and his own received him not. The first thing they did with Jesus was to make him the scapegoat and then drive him outside the camp. They took him from the chambers of Herod to the chambers of Pilate and they gave him into the hands of those who were unclean, those who were "outside the camp." Then he was killed by a means that was not a Jewish means of execution. He was killed with the stigma of being unclean because of the Gentile means of execution. Remember what Paul said in Galatians: "Cursed is everyone who is hanged on a tree."

Jesus was not taken to the temple to be offered on the altar of burnt sacrifice as the perfect sacrifice once for all, given to the Father to end the Day of the Atonement. Jesus was taken outside the city of Zion. They made him carry his pagan cross, his Gentile death weapon, outside the Holy City limits, to Golgotha, to be crucified and destroyed outside the camp. He was attached to the tree. As he hung upon the tree, we read that darkness covered the earth (cf. Matt. 27:45). The light of the countenance of God was removed from Jesus. The world was filled with darkness and it was the middle of the day. But, in that moment in human history, the sun did not shine. The radiance of the fire that came from the Son—this One who was in perfect unity with the Father, who was in the beginning with God and was God—was extinguished. God turned his back on Jesus Christ. It was not from the nails, but from the curse that Jesus cried, "My God, my God, why have you forsaken me?"(Matt. 27:46).

When I was ordained, I had the opportunity to choose my hymn of ordination. On that occasion, I of course chose my favorite hymn, "'Tis Midnight and on Olive's Brow." To me, it is the most poignant hymn of the passion of Jesus that has ever been written, but there is one phrase that should catch our attention. It is that little phrase, in the third stanza, that says that Jesus was not forsaken by his God. But, if Jesus was not forsaken by his God, then you and I are standing alone in our wretchedness before the Father's judgment, and we will have to be measured by the law of works. This is what Albert Schweitzer could never understand. As he looked at the cross and read the words of Jesus' cry, he reasoned that Jesus expected deliverance and didn't get it. So he cried out in lamentation and died in disillusionment. "What a noble effort, Jesus! We applaud your love and your self-sacrifice to no end, but too bad that you never made it." This was Schweitzer's view.

Against this view, we understand that Jesus cried out the way he did because he was forsaken by the living God on the cross. God had essentially said to his people, "I set before you, O Israel, blessing and curse." What he was saying was, "My presence or my absence, the choice is yours. If you obey my law, you will know my presence and see my face. If you sin against that law I will forsake you, for you have forsaken me." That, in a nutshell, is the covenant. If we break the covenant, we have nothing to look forward to but the curse of God, unless the Son of Glory, as our substitute, drinks the cup. The lights are turned out and he screams as he is cursed in our place. That was hell.

Calvin was asked, "Do you believe that Jesus descended into hell?" "Oh yes," was his reply. The Apostles' Creed reads like this: "Suffered under Pontius Pilate, was crucified, dead, and buried; he descended into hell." But when, according to Calvin, was the descent into hell? When Jesus went out into the wilderness and was driven outside the camp, then the demand of God's justice was satisfied. Only then did God turn the lights back on. It was after this that Jesus said, "It is finished. Father, into your hands I commit my spirit" (cf. John 20:21; Luke 23:46). Atonement is over, the price has been paid, satisfaction has been given, and death has no hold on him anymore. On Calvin's view, the descent into hell mentioned in the Creed came when Jesus was bearing the sins of his people on the cross.

But to return to the drama of the atonement, it was only a matter of time until God broke the bonds of death and delivered his Son for the world to see. Because of this, we can dance and sing and be free. The ultimate scapegoat found his way back out of the wilderness and went into the temple and he took the veil and he ripped it down. And he said, "Come, you who are blessed by my Father, inherit the kingdom prepared for you from the foundation of the world." God, the Holy Spirit, takes this work and he begins to apply it to us. There is only one reason under heaven why this happens. There is only one reason why anyone is in the kingdom of God. It has to do with satisfaction—not the satisfaction of the Father, but the satisfaction *of the Son*.

He looks at you and says, "It was worth it to go to hell. You are my fruit. The Father is satisfied and I am satisfied." And God pity you if you are not satisfied with redemption like that.

6

The Language of
the Marketplace

JAMES M. BOICE

*And the L*ORD *said to me, "Go again, love a
woman who is loved by another man and is an
adulteress, even as the L*ORD *loves the children of
Israel, though they turn to other gods and love cakes
of raisins." So I bought her for fifteen shekels of
silver and a homer and a lethech of barley.*
—Hosea 3:1–2

WHAT COMES TO MIND when you think of a marketplace? Maybe you think of people hurrying here and there, purchasing whatever it is that they need. Or maybe you think of a crowded market in a distant Middle Eastern land. In either case, you certainly think of things being bought and sold. But, turning to the Bible, I want to focus on what I will call "The Language of the Marketplace." This is really a descriptive title for the word *redemption*, which is what this chapter—and much of the Bible—is about.

Redemption has to do with buying and selling. The word itself derives from two separate Latin words. The first part of the word comes from a Latin word that means "again." The second part comes from a root which means "to buy," so it refers to buying again or, to be more specific in terms of the biblical theology, it is to buy out of the marketplace. Even more specifically, it refers to that which is purchased in the marketplace, so that what is purchased will never have to return there.

Now that we know what the word means, I'd like to give you a definition of redemption that embraces the central aspects of what this word is meant to convey biblically. This, I hope, will help you to remember it, as well as provide a framework for our discussion. I define redemption as deliverance from the bondage of sin by Christ, at the cost of his life, because he loved us. The matter of deliverance that is in the first part of this definition is easy to understand. I have in mind to be delivered from slavery, which is the kind of deliverance that is meant.

This makes me think back to a book I read years ago that was made into a movie a few years later. It was one of the greatest moneymakers in the history of the film industry: *Ben-Hur*. I remember a scene in the movie and a phrase from both the book and the movie, which captures something of the oppression and hopelessness of being a slave. After a very privileged upbringing in Jerusalem, Judah Ben-Hur, the hero of the novel, through a series of misfortunes, is arrested by the Roman powers in Palestine. He is judged and finally condemned to a life serving in one of the Roman galleys. There is this magnificent scene in the galley where Judah, having fallen from his position of privilege, is assigned to the bowels of the ship. There he is, rowing away with all these other condemned men, suffering a hopeless future and expecting to die eventually. He is only hanging on by sheer grit, by the skin of his teeth, and rowing day after day with no relief in sight. The men around him are beginning to express their despair at this kind of dismal existence, and as they vocalize this to the admiral, he explains the reason for their existence in these words: "We keep you alive to serve this ship."

I can't think of anything that better epitomizes the despair of bondage that a slave must feel, or the spiritual bondage that we feel by virtue of our sinfulness. "We keep you alive to serve the ship." In other words, our life is sustained simply so we continue on in the kind of bondage that we would be glad to be rid of, even at the cost of death. Returning to *Ben-Hur*, you may remember the moment when God intervenes. In a battle, the slaves in this particular ship are set free. Judah Ben-Hur rescues the admiral and is later adopted as his son and rises to a position of power and authority once again. This symbolizes what redemption means. It means to be delivered from the bondage in which we find ourselves. If you can understand this on a physical level, you can understand it spiritually. Perhaps for this reason, the idea of redemption touches us so closely.

One of my favorite hymns is Charles Wesley's "And Can It Be That I Should Gain." It contains what is probably my favorite verse of any hymn in the English language. I refer to it as the great verse of deliverance. If you know that hymn and remember those words, you are aware that I am talking about the fourth verse.

Long my imprisoned spirit lay,
fast bound by sin and error's night;
thine eye diffused a quickening ray;
I rose, the dungeon flamed with light;
my chains fell off, my heart was free,
I rose, went forth, and followed thee.

That's what it means to be redeemed in the first sense, and this is one reason why it speaks to us so clearly.

Let's return to our definition again and examine the second part, "deliverance from the bondage of sin by Christ." Here is the second reason why this is a particularly delightful idea and why it should be commended warmly to every Christian. Paul spells out the basis of our salvation clearly using three key terms, which are often used to describe what happens when God saves us. "Being justified as a gift by His grace through the redemption which is in Christ Jesus; whom God displayed publicly as a propitiation in His blood through faith" (Rom. 3:24–25, NASB).

Three words in this passage describe what the various persons involved (in what I will call "the salvation triangle," see chapter 3) do or receive in the matter of salvation. We contribute nothing to salvation. God the Father is the recipient of one aspect, and he is the source of the other. He is propitiated and justifies, while the Lord Jesus Christ is both the source of propitiation to the Father and redemption to us. The point is that these three terms, justification, propitiation, and redemption, are all important. It is redemption alone that speaks of what the Lord Jesus Christ does on our behalf through his death. He redeems us. When we speak of being delivered from the bondage of sin by Christ, our love for Christ rejoices on the basis of what he's done. The way to learn what is really at the heart of the religious experience of the Christian church is to look, not at the theology books, but at the hymnbooks. Look at the hymns that speak of our Lord Jesus Christ as the Redeemer—and of his work of redemption—if you want to learn the heart of the Christian's experience.

The third part of my definition explains that redemption is the deliverance from the bondage of our sin by Christ at the cost of his life. Here I run into an area where many biblical scholars, though they would have undoubtedly followed everything I have said up to this point, nevertheless would depart. We are talking about cost, and many people today object to this kind of terminology. In a similar fashion, they object to the idea of propitiation because it involves the wrath of God, which is thought to be an ignoble concept. Therefore, the idea of propitiation in their thinking is changed to expiation, which is very different. In the same way, some have protested against this understanding of redemption involving a price.

The objection is that if God saves us the cost of a price—whatever that price may be—then our salvation is not free, and therefore, it's not of grace. And since we all know that we are saved by grace, the notion of cost as it relates to the cross of Christ must be wrong. Therefore, when we talk of redemption we have to talk about it not so much as redemption by the payment of a price but simply and exclusively in terms of deliverance.

If I were playing devil's advocate, I could find passages and descriptions that seem to support this line of thinking. For example, in Luke 24:13–31, when the disciples were making their way home after the resurrection, our Lord appeared to them. As Jesus began to interrogate them, they said to him, "Don't you know what happened? Why, there was a great prophet named Jesus. He came from Nazareth, and he did mighty acts among the people. He was a great teacher. You know in these last days he was taken by the rulers of the people, tried, condemned, and was crucified.

Now he is dead. It's all over." They had hoped that it would be this one who should have redeemed Israel. Notice that in this account they use the word *redemption*, because that is what Jesus was doing; he was redeeming Israel upon the cross. The reason they use that word, in that way, is because they meant it, not in the spiritual sense of a redemption by a price, but as deliverance. They had hoped that this was the Messiah who would drive out the Romans. From this perspective, I could take this incident and its use of the word *redemption* to argue that in New Testament times it no longer had the meaning that is sometimes given to it by Reformed and other biblical theologians.

The obvious problem with this approach, however, is that the amassed disciples misunderstood what Christ came to do. Luke tells us that, in response to the disciples' mistaken understanding of his coming, Jesus began to unfold for them the things from the Word of God concerning himself. He showed how it was necessary that he should suffer these things and be delivered into the hands of wicked men, be crucified, slain, and raised on the third day so that repentance from sin and forgiveness should be proclaimed throughout all the nations. He concludes that they were witnesses of these things. All this is the interpretation of the word *redemption* from the mouth of our Lord. But there are far better reasons for insisting upon the matter of redemption involving a price other than this simple interpretation of Luke 24, which I would like to explore in four points.

First, we must retain this concept of the price of redemption in our understanding because it is the Old Testament idea. All of the New Testament writers who used this word did so with an Old Testament understanding. There is a word *ga'al* and its noun form is *go'el*, which is usually translated in the Old Testament as "kinsman-redeemer" because it contains the idea of redemption. We could best illustrate the concept of the kinsman-redeemer with the great Old Testament example, the book of Ruth. It was a principle in Israel's law that property should remain within a family. To be deprived of property was to be deprived of your share in the land, your inheritance. To lose your land was utterly disastrous, so a provision was made in the law of Israel whereby a man, as the head of his household, could receive back lost property through the obligation placed upon a kinsman. This would mean that if a man fell into debt, and his land was sold to pay off the debt, the duty at some point would fall upon his closest kinsman to buy the land back. He would then be obligated to restore it to the family name in order that the man might not be without his property. This was the process of redemption. Boaz did this in the case of the property that had belonged to the husband of Ruth, and although there was a closer kinsman, the closer kinsman declined the obligation. So Boaz, by prior arrangement with the kinsman, undertook the role of the kinsman-redeemer.

There is a second Hebrew word, *kopher*, that suggests the same thing. *Kopher* is a noun and it refers to a ransom price. Suppose that you are a farmer who has an ill-tempered ox, and your ox gets free one day, wanders down to your neighbor's farm, and kills one of your neighbor's servants. At the very least, this is a crime of negligence. Under Israelite law, if this happened, and it could be proven that you were at fault, it is conceivable (and this is exercising the fullest measure of punishment) that you would have to forfeit your life on behalf of the life that was taken. However, there was an arrangement under Hebrew law that allowed the man who owned the animal to redeem either himself or the animal by payment of the *kopher* if he could make an agreement with the relative of the man who had been killed. In other words, it was a settlement that allowed the guilty party to avoid the full extent of the law by providing an amount of money that would satisfy the wronged party for the loss sustained.

The point I'm making is that the Old Testament background of words like these naturally carried over to the Greek language used by Jews to express what the death of Christ meant. Therefore, we find the same kind of usage involved in New Testament terminology. The basic Greek word for redemption is *lutroo*, which means "to loose." It can mean, in its earliest forms, nothing more than deliverance. But as time went on, and the word developed (as these basic words tended to do in the Greek vocabulary), some of the derivatives took on exclusively the idea of deliverance by the payment of a price.

Second, the notion of cost as it relates to redemption must be maintained because it was a Greek understanding too. We find it in a standard Greek formula for the freeing of slaves, which always had to do with paying a price to one of the gods or goddesses. The formula would go like this: "So and so pays to the Pythian Apollo the sum of so many drachmas for the slave on the condition that the slave shall be set free." The idea of setting a slave free by paying a price for his redemption was fundamental to the entire ancient world.

Third, when we turn to the New Testament, all of the key texts that speak of redemption teach us that a price is always involved. In Matthew 20:28, Jesus says, "The Son of Man came not to be served, but to serve, and to give his life as a ransom for many." Jesus is saying that he is going to buy us out of the slavery of our sin at the cost of his life. First Peter 1:18–19, perhaps the clearest verses in the New Testament regarding this matter, explain that believers know they "were ransomed from the futile ways inherited from [their] forefathers, not with perishable things such as silver or gold, but with the precious blood of Christ, like that of a lamb without blemish or spot." The meaning is absolutely inescapable.

We have to notice very briefly that this word group, which contains the Greek words *lutroo, lutron, lutrosis*, is not the only word group that is used for the idea of redemption in the New Testament, though it's the most important. We also come across the word *agorazo*, which means "to buy." It is related to the Greek word *agora*, which means "the marketplace." We also see the word *exagorazo*, which means "to buy out of the marketplace." As we put all of these words together, what we have portrayed is a magnificent description of the work of the Lord Jesus Christ. This is the work by which he entered into the marketplace of sin, and at the cost of his own life, purchased us for himself so that we might be set free in that glorious liberty, which pertains to the children of God.

Returning to my definition, I have come to my fourth point. Redemption is deliverance from the bondage of our sin by Christ at the cost of his life because he loved us. The love of Christ is a huge topic all on its own, and yet I don't see how we can talk about redemption without discussing it. We can talk about justification, perhaps, without the idea of love, since it is a sort of a legal term. We can talk about victory, perhaps, without love. But you cannot talk about redemption without love, because it is for his great love that Jesus paid the price that he did.

I want to illustrate this aspect of our definition by turning to the story of Hosea. Hosea was a preacher and God came to him on one occasion and said, "Hosea, I want to do something really tremendous in your life. I am going to ask you to marry a woman who is going to be unfaithful to you. I am telling you this in advance because I want you to know why I'm asking you to do it. You are going to marry an unfaithful woman, but you are going to be faithful to her even though she disgraces your love. I am going to use your marriage as an example of Israel's unfaithfulness to me and my faithfulness to them. You are going to play the part of me in this marriage. She is going to play the part of my people, Israel, and she is going to run away and be unfaithful because that's the way my people act in the spiritual marriage that I have established with them. You are going to be faithful because that's the way I am even though my people dishonor my name."

Hosea married a woman named Gomer, and he tells about it in the opening verses of his (somewhat inappropriately denominated) "minor" prophecy. "When the LORD first spoke through Hosea, the LORD said to Hosea, 'Go, take to yourself a wife of whoredom and have children of whoredom, for the land commits great whoredom by forsaking the LORD.' So he went and took Gomer, the daughter of Diblaim, and she conceived and bore him a son" (Hos. 1:2–3).

We don't know (because Hosea doesn't give us all of the details of this relationship) how long he and Gomer lived together happily. But it must have been for a considerable length of time because they had three children—a son, a daughter, and then another son. When these children were born, God intervened to give them symbolic names. He explained that this marriage was an illustration and symbolic of spiritual truth, and therefore, he wanted every aspect of the marriage to symbolize spiritual truth. So Hosea gave the children names that communicate to all who read and understand the story down through the ages of the church what happens when God's people run away from him. The first child was named Jezreel, which in Hebrew means "scattered." Symbolically this meant that the time was coming when, because of their sin, God was going to visit judgment upon his people and scatter them all over the face of the earth. They are still scattered today, and

I believe that's a fulfillment of this prophecy, which we find back here in the first chapter of Hosea.

We must recognize that this text has a far greater application than merely to the Jewish people. Sometimes we treat prophecy in this way and put it in a box that only applies to this particular group and doesn't have anything to do with us. But if we do that with Hosea we miss the great principle that when you run away from God you get in trouble. God doesn't allow you to disobey with impunity. Hosea is the story of God's faithfulness and love, but included in that expression of faith and love is punishment of sin. So, if we think we can run away with impunity, we are sadly mistaken. Another Biblical character, namely Jonah, illustrates this principle well. Jonah ran away from the Lord and he never got to where he was going. And though he paid for his ticket, he didn't get a refund! When you run away from God, you never get where you are going, and you always pay your own bills. But, when you go God's way, you always arrive at your destination free of charge.

With Gomer and Hosea, we see this same principle on another level. If we run away from God, then things will not go well. God is faithful and he guarantees that they won't go well. We think that we are going to satisfy ourselves by seizing the world and its pleasures, but God will make the pleasures of the world turn to dust in the Christian's mouth. Keeping this in mind, we see that the second child was a daughter named Lo-ruhamah. This Hebrew word has two parts. *Lo* means "no" or "not," and *ruhamah* means "pity" or "pitied." God told Hosea to name his daughter Lo-ruhamah because the time was coming when he would not have pity upon the people. God is undoubtedly a pitying and merciful God. But there are times when he will visit judgment upon us for our sin in such a way that will not show pity. God was telling Hosea that judgment will come, and the second name signified that. The third and last child was named Lo-ammi, which means "not my people." God was saying that the time was coming when he would do a new thing. Soon it would be said widely that the Israelites were no longer the people of the living God.

At this point, you might be wondering what happened to the story of God's faithfulness and love. All I have been talking about is judgment, being scattered, not being pitied, and being disowned! How is that a story of God's faithfulness? But we ask this question because we are shortsighted. Human beings always are because we don't know the end of the story. But God wants to increase our vision and tell us the end of the story at the beginning. Hosea 1:10 gives us a glimpse of the glorious ending he has in store. The prophet explains in this verse and the next chapter that God has promised to change his children's names. He is going to change the meaning of Jezreel from "scattered" to "planted," and the name Lo-ruhamah, meaning "not pitied," to Ruhamah, which means "pitied." Finally, Lo-ammi will be changed from "not my people" to Ammi, which means "my people." Hosea 1:10 helps explain what this change of names means and shows us a part of the vision of the future God has shown to Hosea: "And in the place where it was said to them, 'You are not my people,' it shall be said to them, 'Children of the living God.'" The word translated "children" means "people," the *ammi* of the living God.

After all of this begins to come to pass in Hosea's life, his wife, Gomer, catches the eye of another man. She begins to flirt with him and eventually runs off with him, committing adultery and leaving Hosea and the children behind. The meanings of Jezreel, Lo-ruhamah, and Lo-ammi, become clear when we see the downhill course that Gomer chooses. It's downhill spiritually, but it's even downhill in the unbelieving world. We know what happens to a woman who lives this kind of life. One year she will be living with a man who is able to take care of her pretty well. In contemporary terms, we'd say that he is able to provide her with a Cadillac and a mink coat. But the next year, after that man is tired of her and she is forced to live with someone else, she will be living with someone who can't care for her quite as well. Then she'll get an Oldsmobile Cutlass and an artificial fur with a mink collar. The year following that it will be a Toyota, and she'll be wearing a tweed coat. Then she'll be driving around on a motorcycle, and eventually she'll have nothing at all. She won't have enough clothes to keep warm, and she'll be forced to search through the garbage.

This is exactly what happened to Hosea's wife. She sank lower and lower on the social scale of the city, until the time came when she was living with a man who couldn't take care of her. He couldn't provide her with enough food to eat or clothes to wear. We see this and think that it makes sense. If we run away from God, and things go badly, then God is going to say, "You ran away from me—look how wretched it is. Aren't you sorry you ran away?" Isn't that the way we think? Doesn't that seem to follow?

Thankfully, it's not the way God thinks. Sin has its consequences, but what God does at this point is intervene in Gomer's life, just as he intervenes in our lives. God cares for Gomer by instructing Hosea to care for her. At God's command, Hosea buys food and clothing for his adulterous wife so that she won't lack necessities. This must have been a hard and emotional experience for him. It's hard for us to read, but it's there in the Bible. Hosea must have gone to the area of the city where Gomer was living with her lover. I imagine the lover answered the door and Hosea asked, "Are you are the man who is living with Gomer, the daughter of Diblaim?" The man probably answered, "Yes, what business is it of yours?" Hosea may have replied, "Well, I am Hosea, her husband." The man must have drawn back thinking Hosea was there to cause trouble. But Hosea would have continued, "I am not here to cause trouble. I understand that you are not able to take care of her so I bought these things for her. Take them and see that she doesn't lack anything." The lover would have thought to himself, "What a fool this man is!"

To make matters worse, the lover took the things Hosea had bought for Gomer, scoundrel that he was, and he went to her and said, "Look what I brought you!" Hosea must have been hanging around in the shadows to see Gomer throw her arms around the neck of the lover and say, "Oh! My wonderful lover, who provides for me!" Hosea tells us that Gomer didn't know that he was the one who really had provided for her: "For their mother has played the whore; she who conceived them has acted shamefully. For she said, 'I will go after my lovers, who give me my bread and my water, my wool and my flax, my oil and my drink'" (Hos. 2:5). "And she did not know that it was I who gave her the grain, the wine, and the oil, and who lavished on her silver and gold, which they used for Baal" (Hos. 2:8).

God's love is like that. We run away, disgrace his name, and think that we are going to make it on our own, fools that we are. We bring misery upon ourselves, and even as we run, God takes care of us. A moment ago, I mentioned that when we run away, we always pay our bills ourselves. But because God is the Creator and sustains us in our lives—giving us breath even to blaspheme his name—he is always paying the bills in order that we might go on living whether we acknowledge him or not. That's how great God's love is for us.

We've now come to the point for which I have been retelling the story of Hosea. Gomer sank lower and lower on the social scale and eventually she became a slave. Now there were different ways in which a person could become a slave in antiquity. One could become a slave by conquest. For example, when the Athenians tried to attack Sicily back in the time of the Peloponnesian War, they were defeated there and all of the army that was taken at the Battle of Syracuse became slaves. One could become a slave that way. Or, one could become a slave by birth. If your parents were slaves and you were born into that family, you became a slave automatically. Finally, one could become a slave through death.

Presumably, this is how Gomer became a slave, possibly because the man she was with died. She came to the depths of her misery and was sold upon an auction block as a slave in the capital city. Hosea was told by God to go down and buy her, and he describes it vividly. We get a feeling for it from the way he tells it. We also know something about the buying and selling of slaves in antiquity because much was written about it. One thing we learn from these writings is that slaves were always sold naked.

There is a Greek play in which a fat man is put up for sale and while they are bidding on him all his obesity is revealed. The bids are extremely low—ten cents, fifteen cents, twenty cents—and the auctioneers begin to joke with one another. One man says, "Why do you bid twenty cents for that fat slave? Why, as soon as he gets to your home, he is going to eat everything in your house!" The man who bid twenty cents replies, "No, you don't understand. I have a squeaky mill. I am going to cut him and use him for grease." That was considered humorous in a Greek play.

But look at the story from Hosea. A beautiful woman is put up for sale, and her clothes are taken off. In this instance, the bidding is not ten or twenty cents, but one hundred, one hundred and twenty, one hundred and fifty dollars! This is essentially what happened when the men who traded in the marketplace bid for the body of a female slave. That's what happened to Gomer. She was put up for sale, and her clothes were taken off. The men of the city were there to see her in her nakedness and her beauty. They began the bidding and that's when God told Hosea to go down and buy his wife back. One man would have said, "Twelve pieces of silver." Hosea would have said, "Thirteen, fourteen, fifteen pieces of silver." Low bidders are beginning to drop out, but one man is still bidding and says, "Fifteen pieces of silver and a bushel of barley." Hosea replies, "Fifteen pieces of silver and a bushel and a half of barley!" The auctioneer looks around and there are no more bids. "Sold! to Hosea, for fifteen pieces of silver and a bushel and a half of barley."

What happens next is astounding. At this point, Hosea owns his wife. She is his property. He could do anything he wished with her. If he wanted to kill her out of spite, he could have done it. All the people watching the auction might have called him a fool to waste all that money on such a worthless woman. Hosea could have made Gomer endure terrible hardship as a slave. Yet he didn't, because Hosea's love—which is an illustration of the love of God for us—burned in its brightness. What he did was to put her clothes back on her, lead her away into the anonymity of the crowd, and claim his love from her. Here is the way he puts it: "Go again, love a woman who is loved by another man and is an adulteress, even as the LORD loves the children of Israel, though they turn to other gods and love cakes of raisins" (Hos. 3:1). "And I said to her, 'You must dwell as mine for many days. You shall not play the whore, or belong to another man; so will I also be to you'" (Hos. 3:3). That is God's pattern. That is the way God loves us and that is the meaning of redemption.

If we understand redemption—that purchase which lifts the slave out of the marketplace—we understand that this story of

Hosea is our story. We are the slaves sold on the auction block of sin. The world bids for our bodies with fame, wealth, prestige, influence, and power—all the things that are the world's currency. But God sent the Lord Jesus Christ, his Son, into the marketplace, to buy us at the cost of his blood.

Maybe another illustration will help us to understand this. The Father said, "What am I going to bid for these poor, hopeless, enslaved sinners?" And the Lord Jesus Christ replied, "I bid the price of my blood." God the Father said, "Sold! To the Lord Jesus Christ at the price of his blood." There is no greater price than that. We become his and he takes us away and clothes us, not with the robes of our old unrighteousness (which are filthy rags), but with the robes of his own righteousness. And to the Christian he says, "You shall not play the whore, or belong to another man; so will I also be to you." That's how God loves us. That's the meaning of redemption. That's what Jesus Christ did on your behalf. Maybe you've never really understood this. If not, allow the love of the Lord Jesus Christ—the One who bid on your behalf—to draw you to him.

For those of you who know him by grace alone, remember that you were bought with a price. Remember that he also commands us to not play the harlot. Do not flirt with the values of our culture, whatever they may be. You belong to him! Someone may say, "But aren't we set free?" Yes, we are set free; that's what redemption means. But, remember that "for freedom Christ has set us free; stand firm therefore, and do not submit again to a yoke of slavery" (Gal. 5:1). So it is not liberty to sin that God has redeemed us for. Rather, it is a liberty to faithfully love the One who loved us and gave himself for us.

7

Christ, the Sin-Bearer

SINCLAIR FERGUSON

*He was despised and rejected by men; a man of
sorrows, and acquainted with grief; and as one
from whom men hide their faces he was despised,
and we esteemed him not. Surely he has borne our
griefs and carried our sorrows; yet we esteemed him
stricken, smitten by God, and afflicted.*
—Isaiah 53:3–4

THERE IS NOT much from the great Scottish Reformation that has persisted in the present educational system of my homeland. One subject from the Reformation era that always used to be in the curriculum (at least in my school days) was instruction on matters of religious knowledge. This meant that each day would begin with an assembly of the whole school, during which a hymn would be sung, prayer would be made, and Scripture would be read.

I have never forgotten the day when one of my best friends was appointed to read the passage from Isaiah that we are going to examine. He introduced the passage by saying, "The reading this morning is taken from the gospel according to Isaiah." Since he was a close friend of mine, my first reaction was to close my eyes and think, "Oh no! He has goofed!" My second reaction, because I was a young Christian at the time, was to thank God for the illumination that had come, all unexpected, out of the mouth of one of my pagan friends.

Unwittingly, my friend had said precisely what Isaiah chapters 52 and 53 really are: the gospel according to Isaiah. It is the prophet's exposition, in terms of the special revelation and illumination God had given to him, of the significance of the coming of our Savior, Jesus Christ. It is also, as you may or may not know, the passage that even our Lord Jesus himself apparently recalled in his ministry constantly. His mind was saturated by its every phrase; his thinking was dominated by the way in which God intended to inform even him, as he grew in wisdom and knowledge, out of the pages of this passage of Scripture.

Our God intended to inform even the Lord Jesus Christ of the style, character, pattern, and pathway of the ministry that lay before him. And so very often in the gospel narratives we find echoes of Isaiah 53. And in the teaching and preaching of the apostolic church, one finds the apostles constantly returning, in different ways, to the portrait that is given of Christ here, etched out of the pages of Old Testament Scripture. They recognized that here is the great Old Testament portrait of the Savior who was to come. To give just one example, think of what happened when Philip met the Ethiopian eunuch in the desert as he was reading the scroll of Isaiah. The man asked Philip, "Of whom did the prophet speak? Of himself or of some other?" We read in the Acts of the Apostles how Philip began to speak to him about the good news concerning Jesus.

It's in this light that I want us to study this passage together and try to capture something of the way in which it had dominated the thinking of our Lord Jesus Christ. I want us to do this so that we may try to recapture something of the teaching he presumably gave to the two disciples on the road to Emmaus. There, he told them that it was necessary for the Messiah first to suffer and then in the power of God to enter into his glory.

The poem (or song) concerning the suffering servant in Isaiah 52:13 to 53:12 is the fourth of a series of songs or poems in which the strange—and at first shadowy—figure of the servant begins to emerge. This is set in the context of Isaiah's looking towards the exile of the people in Babylon and the restoration of the people by the mighty hand of God. He has already focused attention on the fact that this servant is marked by characteristics that we now know are fulfilled only in our Lord Jesus Christ. We find Isaiah's descriptions in chapters 42, 49, and 50, which portray various aspects of the way in which the character of our Lord Jesus would emerge in the Gospels. The pattern of Jesus' ministry would be laid down for him by God's Word.

It is in the course of this teaching that Isaiah proclaims the coming judgment of God upon his own people and their exile in the far country of Babylon. The people were going to experience what it would be like to be unable to sing the Lord's song in an alien land. But, in general, Isaiah is preaching a message of comfort, consolation, and salvation to the people of God. He wrote with the knowledge that God would come again and visit his people to bring them out of their exile. God would introduce the powerful work of a new exodus, in which his people would be brought back to the land of promise, no longer to be a prodigal people in a far country. It seems that it is in the midst of this kind of revelation that Isaiah wrote chapters 52 and 53.

Also, this took place in the context of the Lord showing him about the deep and radical nature of his own sinfulness. This happened when he saw God in the temple (cf. Isa. 6:1–10). But God also began to unveil to the prophet that the real exile of man is far more radical then the exile of the people of God in Babylon. This being the case, God also showed Isaiah that the real deliverance that man needs is far more costly than the exodus that God would work out in the coming decades to bring the people back to the Promised Land.

Consequently, out of the shadows of Isaiah's wrestling with the word of God concerning the immediate future of the people, there begins to stand this shadowy figure of the servant of the Lord, the One who will be the ultimate deliverer of God's people. He will not only geographically save them and deliver them, but will spiritually, permanently, and gloriously save them. This is the One set forward in the first of the poems concerning the servant, found in Isaiah 42:1. This would be the servant whom the Lord would uphold in the course of his ministry.

By the time we come to the fourth of the servant songs, the spotlight has fallen upon the servant once again. In chapter 52:13, we read, "Behold, my servant shall act wisely; he shall be high and lifted up, and shall be exalted." At this point, the picture that is now clearly before us is a picture not only of the graciousness of the servant, but ultimately the suffering of the servant. This is because he has come to deliver the people by being their sin-bearer. For this reason, one older commentator has said that this passage seems as though it were written at the foot of the cross of Calvary.

The poem itself, found in chapters 52 and 53, is (and you will certainly see this if you have a modern text of the Old Testament) divided into five stanzas and each stanza has three verses. The stanzas—indeed, the whole poem—are carefully structured so that we will not miss what Isaiah's ultimate focus is. Stanzas 1 and 5 describe the servant's exaltation following his humiliation. Stanzas 2 and 4 describe the servant's multifaceted suffering. Finally, stanza 3, which stands like the jewel in the crown of the poem, the centerpiece of the melody of the entire whole, explains the significance of his ministry. There we read these familiar words, "Surely he has borne our griefs and carried our sorrows; yet we esteemed him stricken, smitten by God, and afflicted" (Isa. 53:4).

It's very striking to notice the way in which Isaiah introduces us to this theme. He prepares us mentally, psychologically, and spiritually for what is to come by setting before us, in the mouth of God, the glory of the servant who has come to suffer. Look at what the prophet says, for example, in 52:15. So regal is the servant that he will leave royalty speechless in his presence; kings will shut their mouths because of him. Such is his influence that he will sprinkle many nations. His power will be unlimited; the extent of his influence and authority will be without geographical boundary, and yet, in the very same breath, the Lord is revealing that this is so because the servant's exaltation will be preceded by gross disfigurement. To paraphrase that section, "Just as there were many who were appalled at him, his appearance was disfigured beyond that of any man, and his form marred beyond human likeness."

So, on the one hand, his influence will be geographically unlimited and will reach to silence the mouths of those who sit upon the thrones of the nations' exaltation. On the other hand, this exaltation is rooted in the most profound humiliation. Isaiah speaks of glory and majesty that is rooted in profound agony. He goes on to say, at the beginning of chapter 53, that it is utterly astonishing that his influence is unlimited though his suffering is indescribable. So astonishing is this fact that it will take divine revelation and illumination for men and women even to begin to understand how these two things belong together. Why is it that the exalted One must so grievously suffer? And how is it that the suffering One so gloriously exalted is so appalling that the prophet tells us it will require divine illumination to understand? Why is it, we are tempted to ask, that this would remain a mystery forever, a closed book to the human race, apart from divine revelation?

Isaiah himself asked these kinds of questions: "Who has believed what he has heard from us? And to whom has the arm of the LORD been revealed?" (Isa. 53:1). It takes divine illumination to grasp the message of the gospel. That is what Isaiah answers. This is because the One to whom the prophet's heart (and ours) is attached, by grace and faith, is persistently described in the course of the previous passage as One who is rejected. He is humiliated and suffers and bears judgment (cf. Isa. 53:6, 8, 10) And what Isaiah wants the people to see—and what the Spirit wants us to recognize through this portion of God's Word—is that our Lord Jesus Christ, as the Savior of men, saves precisely because he is the sin-bearer.

Without Jesus Christ bearing our sin, there is no salvation. The very reason for his suffering and agony, the very reason he goes to the cross of Calvary, and the very reason he is marred beyond human recognition was so that he might be the sin-bearer of men and women. And it is to this that Isaiah draws our attention, to answer, in a very general way, that most vexing of questions: how is it that this coming One will become our sin-bearer and Savior? The general answer is given in the title with which he describes the coming Lord.

In Isaiah 52:13, you will notice (it is repeated again in 53:11) that the servant is qualified to be the Savior. It is because he epitomizes what it means to be the servant of the Lord that he is qualified to save men and women. This is simply another way of saying that it is by his obedience that our Lord Jesus Christ becomes our Savior. This has traditionally been described two ways. The first is called the active obedience of Christ, which describes his life of fellowship with God and service to God, by which he provides for us a life of perfect righteousness, to be given to us in the grace of the gospel. The second is his passive obedience (though there is nothing passive about it, in the usual sense of that word), which describes our Lord's suffering in bearing the burden and the curse, going to the cross and suffering agony, as he stands in the place of sinners. When we take these servant songs together, we discover that this is exactly what Isaiah is saying about the servant. He is setting him before us in terms of his obedience to the Father on behalf of others.

So we find here some of the most beautiful things in the whole of Scripture about the active obedience of our Lord Jesus Christ. For example, listen to the words that come from the lips of the servant of the Lord.

> The Lord GOD has given me
>   the tongue of those who are taught,
> that I may know how to sustain with a word
>   him who is weary.
> Morning by morning he awakens;
>   he awakens my ear
>   to hear as those who are taught.
> The Lord GOD has opened my ear,
>   and I was not rebellious;
>   I turned not backward. (Isa. 50:4–5)

Then the prophet begins to speak about his passive obedience.

> I gave my back to those who strike,
>   and my cheeks to those who pull out the beard;
> I hid not my face
>   from disgrace and spitting.
>
> But the Lord GOD helps me;
>   therefore I have not been disgraced;
> therefore I have set my face like a flint,
>   and I know that I shall not be put to shame. (Isa. 50:6–7)

So having given us in this song, and in previous songs, a most exquisite description of the active obedience of our Savior throughout the whole course of his ministry—preparing himself to be the perfect spotless Lamb of God to be offered on the altar of Calvary—Isaiah now focuses his attention where the New Testament itself will focus our attention: on the suffering of the servant. Jesus came not only to live a life of obedience on our behalf, but also to make his soul an offering for our sin. It is in this capacity that Isaiah invites us to follow the pathway of the servant's ministry. This pathway involves a gigantic step downwards in humility, followed by a gigantic step downwards in humiliation, followed by an extraordinary leap upwards in exaltation and glory. I want to focus our attention especially on these two great, giant steps downward that the gracious servant of the Lord takes in order to be our sin-bearer.

The first of the two steps is found in Isaiah 53:2–3 and describes the servant's identification with us. It is a description of how our Lord Jesus would take on our frail flesh in his Incarnation. Verse 2 reads, "For he grew up before him like a young plant, and like a root out of dry ground." It is a moving description of the sorrows that Jesus would experience as he would share in our infirmities. It is a moving encapsulation of what Paul would express very concretely in Romans 8:3: "For God has done what the law, weakened by the flesh, could not do. By sending his own Son in the likeness of sinful flesh and for sin, he condemned sin in the flesh."

Isaiah, in this mysterious revelation, is beginning to sense the extraordinary wonder of the incarnation of the Son of God, as Jesus qualified himself to be our Savior. The prophet is describing what Paul again is going to describe in Philippians 2:7–8: "But [he] made himself nothing, taking the form of a servant, being born in the likeness of men. And being found in human form, he humbled himself by becoming obedient to the point of death, even death on a cross." Isaiah and Paul both describe our Lord as One whose heart would beat in time with ours; who, in his own weaknesses, would be able to identify with our weaknesses. Who, in his experience of temptation, would be able to identify with our experience of temptation, and who, in his sorrows, grief, and mourning, would be able to identify with our sorrow, grief, and mourning.

Although we already know from the song that this servant is to be highly exalted, the insignia of that exaltation are, for the moment, hidden from our eyes, and all we see is his complete identification with sinful men and women, yet sinless himself. Apart from sin, he is exactly as we are, feeling our infirmities, knowing our crises, and experiencing what it is to be raised in the least likely of environments for spiritual blessing, as a root out of dry ground. He knows what it is to be without either the beauty or the majesty that would attract others to him. Of course, it is this that is taken up in so many ways in the narrative of the Gospels.

The Gospels form a kind of commentary on the beauty of Isaiah's words that describe the empathy of our Lord Jesus Christ in bearing the infirmities of others. For instance, Jesus identifies himself with the leper by taking on his ritual uncleanness. He embraces the fallen and the broken ones. He dwells among the publicans, the sinners, the harlots, and the outcast of society, as well as meets eyeball to eyeball with the rich, the glorious, and the finest of society. Our Lord Jesus comes in order to bear our very flesh, to become one of us apart from sin. This is important for at least two reasons.

First, because of the very nature of the fall. We see something of this in the great parallel that Paul draws between the first Adam and the last Adam in Romans 5:12–21. Paul teaches that God deals with men and women in terms of two heads of humanity. Adam represents the head of the old humanity and Christ the head of the new humanity. Yes, we are sinners individually, and we are saved individually. But undergirding our sin and the transformation that works in our lives is God's dealing with these two men in history—Adam and Jesus Christ. Ultimately, the reason why our Lord Jesus is able to be absolutely one with sinners, and yet remain sinless, is for the very reason that Paul indicates in Romans 5. That is to say, if there is to be a restoration of man after the fall, then it must begin where the fall left us. If we have fallen in Adam, then we must not only be saved through the one man Jesus Christ, but we must be saved through Jesus Christ in the reality of his humanity. Thus, salvation—the restoration of man to God by his grace—does not take place by some easy divine fiat, but begins to take place from within the very pit into which man has sunk by his sin.

Jesus Christ comes into the world and takes on our flesh as the second man through whom God would deal with entire groups of men and women. The last Adam would accomplish the work on our behalf that we could not accomplish ourselves. But it would have to be accomplished within our flesh and blood, and it would have to last forevermore. Isaiah begins to intuit that our Lord Jesus will take flesh and blood. Do you remember how the writer to the Hebrews puts it? "Since therefore the children share in flesh and blood, he himself likewise partook of the same things, that through death he might destroy the one who has the power of death, that is, the devil, and deliver all those who through fear of death were subject to lifelong slavery" (Heb. 2:14–15).

But there is another reason why this focus on Christ's identification with us is so vital for us to grasp. It's not only for the theological reason or so that we may understand the way in which God has constructed his plan of salvation. But it's because we must be persuaded that God really does intend to save us. We must be aware that sin not only separates us from God, but also deceives us about the nature of our hard hearts and the gracious nature of God. Our sinful hearts deceive us about the very nature of God himself. That's what Satan was really after in the Garden of Eden. Formally, the temptation was to repudiate the word of God, but materially, the temptation was to deny the grace of God, the lavishness of God, the trustworthiness of God, and the kindness of God. By nature, none of us trust God as we ought. All of our instincts are to mistrust him because we fear him. We have an instinct that God is against us, and it is in this context that our Lord Jesus Christ says, "Whoever has seen me has seen the Father" (John 14:9).

And what, Jesus asks, have you seen in me? You have seen me take on your flesh, experience your temptations far beyond any experience of temptation you have ever had, and go into the depths of suffering that you have never known. It is almost as if Jesus asks, "Don't you see what it is that God is revealing to you through me? He is showing you how deeply he loves you. He is showing you how deeply he identifies himself with you in his compassion and his passionate concern for you. He is opening his heart to you by all the wounds of my flesh." Jesus is saying that God is opening his heart to you to teach you how profoundly he cares for you.

Because of the nature of the fall and the effect of sin on our very thinking about God, Jesus comes. Isaiah very poignantly says—and take this into your soul—that Jesus may chiefly be described as "a man of sorrows, and acquainted with grief" (Isa. 53:3). This speaks with great eloquence to us when we consider what Isaiah has already said in the first of these glorious songs.

> He will not cry aloud or lift up his voice,
> or make it heard in the street;
> a bruised reed he will not break,
> and a faintly burning wick he will not quench;
> he will faithfully bring forth justice." (Isa. 42:2–3)

Here is the significance of the Savior's identification with us in our flesh: that he might persuade us that he provides the salvation we require and is the very Savior that we need.

This brings us to the second step in what Isaiah describes about the servant's suffering. The first step was the servant's identification with us. The second step is Isaiah's exposition of the servant's suffering for us. It's clear from these verses that the servant comes to share in our suffering. But Isaiah also makes it clear that he comes to bear a suffering that is uniquely his.

Notice the multifaceted way in which his suffering is described. The servant experiences violence. He is stricken down. He is pierced through. It is also profoundly physical, and he is *wounded*, says Isaiah (cf. 53:5). It has been said that every category of wound known to medical science would have been found somewhere on the dead body of our Savior when it was brought down from the cross. He was deeply, physically wounded, says Isaiah; he was marred beyond human semblance. His sufferings were fatal. He was cut off physically; to borrow the symbolism of the sign and seal, he was totally circumcised in himself and cut off from the land of the living.

We sometimes say (because in some contexts it's important that we do say it) that Scripture doesn't focus on the physical sufferings of our Savior. But Scripture does make the physical character of his sufferings abundantly plain to underline the reality of his sufferings. The apostle Peter especially does this in 1 Peter 2:24–25 as he thinks about his dear Lord Jesus Christ. He says that Jesus was the One who "himself bore our sins in his body on the tree." That body that was so precious to Simon Peter was the body that was mutilated, physically broken, wounded, pierced, and crushed. This shows the depth of his sufferings for the sinners for whom he had come to make atonement. Because our minds are so poor and frail, we rightly discuss the theories of the atonement. But we must always remember that the atonement is not a theory. It wasn't a theory that died for us on the cross. It was a man who took our very physical nature himself in his own body.

Jesus' body bore our sins on the tree, and it was a horrible, bloody, fatal, and physical reality. The New Testament tells us this to underscore the extent of the servant's service on our behalf (cf. Phil. 2:5–11). Not only did he take the form of a man and humble himself to wear the garb of a servant, but he also became obedient. He even became obedient unto the ghastly death of the cross for our sakes. We see that the whole point was to emphasize how full, complete, and extensive was the servant's obedience to the Father on our behalf. Even when his body is marred beyond human semblance, he bows himself down and says, "For the sake of the salvation of sinners, my Father, let your will be done."

But even in this preview of the cross, Isaiah does not miss that the deepest sufferings of the servant are ultimately spiritual. The reconciliation he accomplishes is achieved not merely by his physical sufferings, but by his entry into alienation from God. He comes down into the depths of our sinful alienation from God and bears the many and varied consequences. He was despised. They laughed at him to scorn. He was rejected. The glorious Son of God is described by the prophet as having no majesty in him to attract us to him. He is held to be utterly without esteem. He is oppressed, and he is crushed. And this is the very thing that echoes forward into the Gospels. We read there that our Lord Jesus said to his disciples, as he went to the garden of Gethsemane, "My soul is very sorrowful, even to death"(Mark 14:34). Mark also tells us in this chapter that Jesus was distressed and deeply troubled in the garden and uses language that is somewhat unique in the New Testament. One commentator described it as the confused, restless, half-distracted state, which is produced by physical derangement or by mental illness. It's a picture of Jesus reeling under the weight of what he is to experience. It's a fulfillment of the messianic psalms that speak about the waters pouring over him and drowning him in their power.

But Isaiah has not yet finished. If the servant's sufferings are violent, physical, fatal, and spiritual, then they are penal. They are a penalty. If death is the wages of sin, then in this death, above all other deaths, the bill for sin is being presented to the servant. Isaiah makes it clear that

He was wounded for our transgressions;
    he was crushed for our iniquities;

upon him was the chastisement that brought us peace,
　　and with his stripes we are healed.
All we like sheep have gone astray;
　　we have turned—every one—to his own way;
and the LORD has laid on him
　　the iniquity of us all. (Isa. 53:5–6)

There are three words that summarize all that Isaiah has to say about the penal character of the servant's death. The first is *expiation*. This means that the penalty is paid in order to take away our guiltiness before God. Isaiah even says this in verse 10: "It was the will of the LORD to crush him; he has put him to grief; when his soul makes an offering for guilt." He will be offered for the guilt of the sin of others in order to take away that guiltiness. The servant was wounded for transgressions and acts of rebellion. It was for our iniquity, our inner perversity, the twistedness of our nature, and our rebellion against God. Isaiah tells us that the servant was bruised, wounded, and chastised to deal with the displeasure of God, which is the inevitable result of our guilt. He bore the stripes to his own body to heal us of the disease of our sin and to loose our souls from its awful bondage. Every stripe, every wound, every moment of crushing—all of that is the payment of the bill for the wages of sin. It was all to pay the penalty price for our guilt. He pays it all. It's a work of expiation.

But the penal work of the servant is also a work of substitution. Here is the reason for his suffering. Here is the consequence of his bearing guilt. The piercing was for our transgressions. The bruising was for our iniquities. The chastisement was for our peace. The stripes were because we needed healing, because we've gone astray and turned to our own way. Thus, the iniquities laid upon him were ours. As the hymn writer says, "In my place condemned he stood, sealed my pardon with his blood."[1]

This work of substitution is frequently illustrated in Scripture. For example, there's the Day of Atonement ceremony. Two goats were taken, lots were drawn, and one of them was slain as a sacrificial offering for the sin of the people. The other had the sin of the people confessed over it and then was taken outside of the camp to wander alone in the wilderness, bearing not its own guilt, but the guilt of the people. This is exactly what Isaiah says is taking place on the cross. On the one hand, the servant goes outside of the camp into the place of barrenness and alienation, forsaken by both man and God. On the other hand, he offers himself up as a sacrifice to bear in his body and soul, the punishment of our guilt. This is why when charges are brought against our Lord Jesus in the Gospels, in every single instance, he is declared to be innocent. It is as though the gospel writers are saying to us, "Don't you have eyes to see what's happening here? Don't you understand the drama that's being played out here?" Although Jesus is repeatedly declared innocent, he pays the penalty because, according to Isaiah, he was wounded for our transgressions and bruised for our iniquities. It was a work, then, of expiation of guilt and of substitution for sinners.

Lastly, the servant's work is a work of propitiation of God. Here we come to the very heart of the matter. Expiation deals with the offense and the guilt. Propitiation deals with the offended One and his wrath. We see how this begins to emerge with what is said here. Isaiah tells us that this is why kings will shut their mouths because of him. And this is what is so utterly unprecedented about the suffering of this particular sufferer. Look at

1. "Man of Sorrows, What a Name." Words and Music: Philip P. Bliss, 1875.

verses 4, 6, and 10. Over and over again, we are brought into the very heart of the mystery of the outworking of our redemption. On the cross of Calvary, our Lord Jesus Christ not only dealt with our guilt, but also exhausted in himself the wrath of God, which was burning against the sin of those for whom he was dying.

This is so beautifully portrayed in the Passion narratives. See Jesus in the upper room giving to his disciples the cup of his own fellowship with God. He says to them, "Take this cup of blessing and fellowship and drink from it, all of you. Do this until I come again and drink it with you in my Father's kingdom" (cf. Matt. 26:27–29). Behold him as he goes out into the garden of Gethsemane and begins to take from his Father's hand a cup from which he shrinks. Hear him cry, "Oh my Father, if it's possible, let this cup—this cup that was described in the prophetic writings as the cup of the judgment and wrath of God against the sin and ungodliness of the nations, the outpouring of the wrath of God against their iniquities—let it pass from me!" (cf. Mark 14:35–36). He was going to take, drink, and consume the cup of God's wrath—and the hand that was going to put it into his hand was the hand of his own Father. It is no wonder that he cried out on the cross, "My God, my God, I am forsaken! Why, why?" And the answer was that God the Father made the iniquity of us all to fall upon Jesus, his Son, our sin-bearer.

It is because of this that Isaiah leads us to the third great step in this passage. Because of the magnitude of his suffering for us, by which sufferings we are redeemed forevermore, Isaiah gives us a glimpse of the servant's exaltation to the right hand of God. We know that the servant's sacrifice for our sins is acceptable because God exalted him. In chapter 53, Isaiah tells us that "when his soul makes an offering for guilt, he shall see his offspring; he shall prolong his days" (v.10). "Out of the anguish of his soul he shall see and be satisfied" (v. 11). The Father "will divide him a portion with the many, and he shall divide the spoil with the strong" (v. 12). God demonstrated his acceptance of the sacrifice by raising the servant from the dead so that he would not be held as a captive by death but might enter into the light of life in a new way. God has demonstrated his satisfaction with the sacrifice of his Son by exalting him to his right hand and giving him the name that is above every name. Oh, the spoils of his triumph on the cross!

We see Jesus in all the glory of what theologians call the *munus triplex*, the three-fold office of our Savior. Jesus became a humiliated prophet who did not open his mouth. He became a humiliated priest who was offered as the sacrifice for guilt. He became a humiliated king so that there was no majesty in him to attract us. Because his work has ended, his mission was accomplished, and his sacrifice was accepted. Thus, God has raised him up and he is now the exalted prophet before whom even kings will shut their mouths and listen. He is the exalted priest who will sprinkle the nations with his sacrificial blood, cleanse them, and make them a fellowship of priests unto God, his Father. He is the exalted king who has returned from battle victorious in his splendor and entered into the majesty of the right hand of God. He has received the spoils of war. "Ask of me," says the Father, "and I will make you the very nations as your inheritance" (cf. Ps. 2:8).

The same truth is given to us from the lips of the apostle Peter, in his tremendous sermon in Acts 5:31. "God exalted him at his right hand as Leader and Savior, to give repentance to Israel and forgiveness of sins." Beloved, let us pause together and ask with the apostle Paul (who undoubtedly was thinking of this passage in Acts),

What then shall we say to these things? If God is for us, who can be against us? He who did not spare his own Son but gave him up for us all, how will he not also with him graciously give us all things? Who shall bring any charge against God's elect? It is God who justifies. Who is to condemn? Christ Jesus is the one who died—more than that, who was raised—who is at the right hand of God, who indeed is interceding for us. (Rom. 8:31–34)

When you realize all of this, my dear friend, you will sing with the hymn writer, "Amazing love, how can it be that thou my God shouldst die for me?"[2]

---

2. "And Can It Be That I Should Gain." Words: Charles Wesley, 1738. Music: Thomas Campbell, 1825.

8

Preaching the Cross

ALISTAIR BEGG

For Jews demand signs and Greeks seek wisdom,
but we preach Christ crucified, a stumbling block
to Jews and folly to Gentiles, but to those who are
called, both Jews and Greeks, Christ the power of
God and the wisdom of God. For the foolishness of
God is wiser than men, and the weakness of God is
stronger than men. —1 Corinthians 1:22–25

WITHOUT THE CROSS of Jesus Christ there is no gospel. There simply is no good news without the cross. Indeed, any attempt to preach the gospel, minus the cross, is to offer people a placebo rather than the very medicine that they require. To be sure, in the taking of the placebo, they may feel that it has done them some good. But, if we have not really explained to them the meaning and purpose of the cross, then we have neither convinced them of their problem, nor have we been able to convey to them the biblical solution. How can God pardon sinners without encouraging sin? How can he simultaneously show justice in punishment but mercy in pardoning? How can he turn his enemies into his friends and bind them to him in eternal love? How can he admit men and woman into heaven without spoiling the holiness of heaven? The answer to all of those questions is in the cross of the Lord Jesus Christ. As foolish as it seems to those who are perishing, to those who are being saved it is the very power of God, as our text demonstrates.

To preach the cross is to explain its necessity, its meaning, and its consequences, in order that at least two things will happen. First, it is preached so that God's people may constantly glory in it. We dare not view the cross as simply a point of static engagement, lost somewhere in the remote history of our spiritual pilgrimage. Rather, the cross must be, for the genuine believer, that ongoing and engaging dynamic of all Christian living. The preaching of the cross is most necessary for the people of God in order that they might glory in the cross. Secondly, it is to be preached in order that unconverted sinners may be humbled by it and brought to faith in the Lord Jesus Christ.

We must see how central the emphasis on the cross really is in our theology, preaching, worship, and witness. Both the reading of Scripture and church history suggest strongly that there is a direct correlation between usefulness under God and the proclamation of the cross of Christ. It suggests that those in the apostolic record, whose ministries were used and owned of God, were those who proclaimed unequivocally the message of the cross. There is a direct link between men who proclaimed the cross in all of its glory and men who were singularly used by God, both in evangelism and in the encouraging of God's people.

Here are a couple of illustrations, both from my homeland. I was brought up in Glasgow, Scotland. I was born there in 1952 and enjoyed all the benefits that were part and parcel of that upbringing. My father would take me regularly to hear various people preach, most of whom I had no interest in hearing as a young boy. But since my father was not in a popularity competition for my affections, he told me exactly where I was going and where I was spending my time! So, on beautiful Saturday afternoons, when I would much rather have been watching soccer or engaging with my friends, he would take me to a Bible conference or some such thing. I went most reluctantly, and I am not sure how I behaved during these events, but I bless God for them now, in retrospect.

One of the individuals who was used of God in Glasgow in my very early days was the Reverend Tom Allen. He was the gentleman who preceded Eric Alexander of St. George's-Tron. Tom Allen's theological training had been interrupted by World War II, and this is how he describes his experience: "I was posted to France as an intelligence officer. One Easter day, I heard an American GI sing the spiritual 'Were You There?' I often think about this American solider having lived the rest of his life, probably forgetting that he sang this song on that Easter Sunday, and never ever knowing the way in which God would use the singing of that song, not only in the life of one of his servants, but also in the evangelizing of a city."

What a tremendous reminder to us that there are no inconsequential tasks in the kingdom! "And on that day," says Tom Allen, "Christ laid hold of my life. I came back, without any background, to resume my interrupted studies for the ministry. The seminary I attended was liberal and modernistic and yet I knew, beyond a shadow of a doubt, the reality of Jesus Christ. In facing the challenges of ministry in the city center of what was the 'Second City' of the British Empire, I was driven to two discoveries, which transformed my ministry. The first was that the preaching of the cross is central. I discovered the meaning of the doctrine of the atonement. The second was the discovery of the authority of the Word of God."

For our second illustration, we move forty-five or fifty miles to the east, to the city of Edinburgh, the capital of Scotland. At the turn of the past century, Alexander Whyte was a famous minister in the city. He was regarded by some as being virtually a monomaniac because of his preaching about sin and salvation. He became aware of the fact that his emphasis on sin and the cross was increasingly unpopular. He tells of how he was tempted to muffle the note of his preaching in order to gain acceptance from his listeners.

One day, while Whyte was walking in the Scottish Highlands, he describes how there seemed to be (what was to him at least) a divine voice. It spoke with all commanding power in his conscience declaring, "Go on and flinch not. Go back and boldly finish the work that has been given you to do. Speak out and fear not. Make them see themselves—at any cost—in God's holy law as in a mirror. Do this, for no one else will do it. No one else will so risk his life and his reputation to do it, and you have not much of either left to risk. Go home and spend what is left of your life in your appointed task of showing my people their sin and their need of my salvation." "And so," said Alexander White, "I will finish as I had begun, I will preach the cross of Jesus Christ."

In the same way, biographers have analyzed the ministry of Charles Haddon Spurgeon from all kinds of angles. All manner of explanations have been given as to his fruitfulness and the excellence and benefits of his proclamation. I put it to you that the answer to it all is aptly summarized on his tombstone. There he has the third verse of the hymn "There is a Fountain Filled with Blood" carved in to his record of his life. The inscription reads, "E'er since by faith I saw the stream Thy flowing wounds supply, Redeeming love has been my theme, And shall be till I die." Spurgeon was driven—compelled—by the absolute sufficiency of Christ, the authority of his Word, and the centrality of the preaching of the cross. The emphasis of these men was nothing other than the emphasis to which all of us who are called to the task of preaching find in the pages of Scripture.

It was surely the emphasis of Paul as he came into the city of Corinth, a significant and decadent city where the citizens were known for the very wanton indulgence of their senses. It was a city in which just about anything went; one could find all kinds of recreational activities and many of them were the very apexes of immorality. Corinth was a city that was at the crossroads of the trading routes of the then known world, and therefore prosperous. It was surrounded by all kinds of religious opportunities and hosted the Isthmian games, which were second only to the Olympic games. It was proud, magnificent, and in many senses I am sure, overpowering.

It is into this city that this converted little Jew walks. After he looked around, we can only imagine that he must have said to himself, "Now, I must be about my Father's business. I must ensure that I stay to the task here." In Acts 18, Luke records for us the way in which the historical events unfolded. It is a wonderful story of how, in the providence of God, Paul hooks up with Priscilla and Aquila. After all, it's always nice to have someone to talk to who has a fair idea of where you are coming from! And these two certainly did because they were tent makers like Paul. He was able to work during the week, and on the Sabbaths, he would go to the synagogue to try and persuade the God-fearing Jews and the surrounding Gentiles of the reality of

Jesus and the significance of his atoning death. After Paul had been doing this for a while, his buddies, Silas and Timothy, arrive from Macedonia. They bring him some resources, and as a result of this support, he is able to preach the cross full time. But it seems that when he "hots it up," his hearers don't like it very much and start abusing him until he is forced to move out of the synagogue. But far from defeated, he simply moves next door to the house of Titius Justus. He hadn't been next door for very long before Crispus, who was the leader of the synagogue, begins to visit. Next, Crispus brings his family over to attend Paul's preaching services and eventually they are all converted. It is a wonderful story isn't it? They throw Paul out, so he goes next door and the guy from the first place becomes a Christian.

In the midst of all of that, God spoke to Paul in a vision and told him three things: don't be afraid; don't be silent; I have many people in this city. If that is not a word for the average preacher in our day, then there is no word! God has ordained men and women to salvation, but he has also ordained the means whereby they will come to salvation. Under his providential overruling, your voice is a significant part in that process. Great is the mystery and yet true is the statement.

The cross of Christ was being declared by Paul in all of its fullness and boldness, and yet with a magnificent humility. It is possible to be bold and humble at the same time, which Paul certainly managed to do. But although he recognized this, he says in 1 Corinthians 1:22 that his message was regarded as foolishness and weakness. However, he knew it to be the very wisdom and power of God: "For the foolishness of God is wiser than man's wisdom and the weakness of God is stronger than man's strength" (1 Cor. 1:25). This kind of thinking was axiomatic for Paul. Until this becomes axiomatic and endemic in the hearts and minds of preachers in our land, we will never preach with deep conviction. But when we come to a deep conviction that God's wisdom is in the strange and seemingly foolish message of the cross, and that in the weakness of this dying Savior is actually the power of God, suddenly vistas of opportunity open before us as we declare this good news. Indeed, without such a conviction, it would be incredible that Paul himself would be caused to adopt such a strange approach.

This is the opposite of what people are saying today. "You are not going to belabor the issue of the cross, are you? There are so many important issues to be dealt with." I had a note given to me just the other day that said, "In light of all of the troubled marriages in our contemporary world, and not least of all in our church, don't you think you would be better off stopping your expositions in the book of Hebrews and addressing the relationships between husbands and wives?" I replied, "No, because the problem is a doctrinal problem before it is a relational problem." Husbands need to understand who Jesus is, why he came, and why he had to die. They need to understand how Christ loved the church because that's how they are supposed to love their wives. I could have given husbands a few little stories about how to love their wives, but only when they know how Christ loved the church will they be able to love their wives. In the same way, only by examining the submissive role of the Son to the Father in the Trinity can we attain a model for a wife's submission to her husband. Therefore, what people actually need is not to rub each other's backs but to hear about the cross of the Lord Jesus Christ. When people aren't getting along in the church, we often think we should talk about interpersonal relationships. But we actually need to preach the cross of Christ. That's what they need.

Paul provides two wonderful illustrations in 1 Corinthians of why he does what he does. Paul explains what he means when he speaks about foolishness and strength, wisdom and weakness. First, he focuses on the people that God uses. To paraphrase 1 Corinthians 1:26–29, Paul asks, "Brothers, think of what you were when you were called. Were you a particularly powerful group? Were you a particularly wise group? Well, no, in fact, not many of you were influential or of noble birth. God chose the foolish things of the world to shame the wise and the weak things of the world to shame the strong. He chose the lowly things, the despised things, and the things that are nothing to nullify the things that are, so that no one may boast before him." In other words, Paul is saying that the principle he has just enunciated about weakness and foolishness is illustrated in the people God chooses. He essentially says, "Just look around the congregation on the Lord's Day morning and see what a funny group we are."

As a pastor, I can say the same thing. You might think that's not very nice, but I am not trying to be nice; I am just trying to be honest. Truly, it's a funny bunch of people in the average church. If you had to come and stand where I stand on a Sunday and look out the people, you'd see that it is a fairly weird bunch. When I look out on them, I don't immediately find myself saying, "Yes! Here is the group that can transform Northeast Ohio!" I usually look out and I think, "Goodness gracious me, with this group?! With her?! With them?!" This is because we Christians don't have political clout. We don't have all the things that people say are necessary if you are going to establish a kingdom. We just have people—all kinds of different people from different places. Sure, we have some interesting ones: there are fighter pilots from the Vietnam War, and those who have an MBA from Harvard, and Cleveland Orchestra people who are prestigious in different circles. But so what? As Paul looks out on this group in Corinth, he sees Mr. and Mrs. Levi and their children wriggling in their seats, being a downright nuisance, and their son Benjamin with his spotty face full of zits, and he wonders, "Am I really going to turn Corinth upside down with this rag bag of humanity?!" That's what he is saying here, it seems to me. Paul tells his church, "If you want to know if God does powerful things in weakness, look at the congregation."

Now, as if that weren't enough, he says, "Think about my preaching." Here is an important display of pastoral wisdom on the part of Paul. Because people would have been inclined to say, "Well, who does he think he is, describing us like that?" Can't you hear them immediately getting on their high horses, "Well! That's the last time Paul comes to our house for dinner! Coming away with that kind of stuff! Vagabond that he is!" But Paul responds, "Let me give you another illustration. Just think about when I showed up in Corinth. Remember how my preaching was? Remember how one group wanted me to do signs and wonders, and another group was really interested in dramatic and eloquent oratory and sophistry? Do you remember that neither group was apparently interested in the preaching of the cross? Did I adopt that kind of 'seeker-sensitive approach' whereby I surveyed the market and tried to figure out what people wanted most? No, I gave them neither. I gave them the one thing that nobody wanted." Paul's approach makes no sense in a market-driven economy. If people want baseballs and you can find a way to make them fast and get them out in the marketplace, you make them. After all, that's what they want, and that's what they will buy. Unfortunately, that is the wisdom of contemporary evangelicalism. But it is not the wisdom of Paul in Corinth.

This is not to say that we engage in obscurity or that we make it difficult for people to cross cultural barriers in our presentation of the good news. But it is to say, that at the very heart of the message that we are called upon to bow under and to proclaim is not being sought by anyone. People are interested in glory, but they are not particularly interested in the cross. They are interested in effectiveness, but they are not interested in impoverishment. They are interested in drama, but they are not interested in the drama of a Galilean carpenter hanging bloodied and beaten on a Judean hill. But, that's exactly what Paul preached, purposely leaving behind eloquence and superior wisdom. He didn't do this because he wasn't eloquent or because he lacked worldly intelligence. It was that he determined that those things would make it more difficult for the people to depend on the message of the cross itself. He understood that it is impossible to establish how clever the preacher is and how great Jesus is at one and the same time. You can't show people how brilliant you are and how wonderful Jesus is simultaneously.

Today, however, there is a kind of preaching that is so apparently effective that it might be completely ineffective. A lot of us preachers are like Polonius in Hamlet. What a pedantic bumbler he was! If one could say something in one sentence he always took ten. The queen cuts him off in one of his speeches and says, "More matter and less art, Polonius!" That's exactly what our congregations are saying to us as those called to preach: "More substance and less art." To put it humorously, as the wee lady in the Wendy's ad asked, "Where's the beef?"

Everywhere I go in this country, people come to me and say, "We are dying in our congregations." From place to place, the message is the same: "We have a good man but our services are full of drama, dancing girls, songs, bells, and smells, but we are dying for the preaching of the Word of God." But is it not so obvious, preachers? It's as clear as the nose on your face. You must read the Bible, explain the Bible, and ask the Holy Spirit to make application of the Bible. And what do you do next Sunday? Read the Bible, explain the Bible, and ask the Holy Spirit to make application of the Bible. You don't have to be a rocket scientist. You only need to understand the English language, have a deep dependence on the truth of God's Word, and have a dramatic desire to stand up with the message of the cross because it is the power of God.

Thinking again on Paul arriving in Corinth, I imagine Mr. Benjamin picking up Paul from the donkey station. As he arrives home, his wife asks, "Levi, what's he like?" "Well," he answers, "he is . . . frankly, he is unimpressive." "Oh he is?" she asks. "Yeah, he is weak, for starters; he is a weak guy, and I can't be sure, but he seems to shake. He is sort of a trembling soul. And when I shook his hand it was all sweaty. And he has these long sentences! Goodness! And, if that weren't bad enough, he seldom ever finishes his sentences!" "Oh!," she says, "how do you think he is going to go down in Corinth?" The answer would've been that he was going to go down really well. Because he went *down*, metaphorically speaking. God said, "I see you here, down; now let me lift you up." The sense of absolute dependence upon God was the very key to the power of Paul's delivery. People probably said, "You know, he doesn't really have much of the stuff that we are looking for, and yet somehow or another God clothes him with his power and we hear God's voice from his strange lips." God delights to hear this.

Alexander Whyte's congregation gives us a wonderful story to illustrate this. The more I tell it, though, the more I start to think it might be apocryphal. Alexander Whyte's pulpit was so significant that young men would regard it as the ultimate accolade to be invited to preach from it. On one occasion, a young chap in Scotland was looking forward to the first opportunity of mounting the pulpit steps at Free St. George's, there in the east end of Prince Street. He was so excited about it that he began to tell people that he had a great message and he couldn't wait to deliver it and, frankly, it was something that the church needed to hear.

Well, the expected day came soon enough. He was on. The door opened, he came up one side of the pulpit steps, and he held his head up and his Bible in the posture that he had been practicing in his bathroom. He strode in, ready to deliver the goods. When the time came for him to preach, he began with his great opening paragraph, which he had honed carefully over a period of some time. He wasn't into it more than a minute when all of the saliva dried up in his mouth. He could hardly get out a sentence and everybody began to merge together into one great mass of humanity. His notes began to fog in front of him, and he was in dire difficulty. He eventually dribbled to a sorry conclusion and then left the pulpit, down the other stairs. But when he walked down this time, he had his chin down in his chest. He was looking at his shoes and he was heading as quickly as he could for the door. An elderly gentleman in the back row turned to his friend and said, "If that young boy had come up the way he went down, he would have gone down the way he came up."

This little story relates one of the greatest detriments to the effective preaching of the cross, namely, us. I am the greatest barrier to its effective preaching in my church. There is too much of me and not enough of him. That's why Paul said and did what he did. Some of us are so smart we are of no use at all. Some of our ministries are wood, hay, and stubble. But because there are numbers that attach to them and there are things that happen in them, we believe them to be silver, jewels, and gold.

Paul explains why he preached the way he did in 1 Corinthians 2:1–5. To paraphrase, he says, "When I preached the cross to you, my purpose was absolutely clear: to make sure that your faith did not rest on men's wisdom but on God's power." The Corinthians loved clever arguments. But Paul recognized that if he had come in with clever arguments, then they would be vulnerable to a more clever argument. Therefore, he explains, "I didn't use clever arguments and I am not here to impress you with wisdom. I have a good background, you know, and I have got a pretty good mind and a fund of stories. But I didn't use any of that."

Paul surely could have impressed them with many things. Take for instance, something like being caught up to the third heaven. Or what about the signs and wonders? They would have been absolutely charming in Corinth. Paul would've been on Corinthian Christian TV in a minute with that one. But he didn't do any of that stuff. In the same way, when we endeavor to show the world how effective, how strong, how wise, and how wonderful we are, we obscure the only message that saves.

And so our cities go on, waiting for the arrival of the kings and the presidents of the world, as if somehow or another, the future of the world rested in Washington, D.C., Beijing, London, or Moscow. But the Bible says, "[He] brings princes to nothing, and makes the rulers of the earth as emptiness" (Isa. 40:23). "'All flesh is like grass and all its glory like the flower of grass. The grass withers, and the flower falls, but the word of the Lord remains forever.' And this word is the good news that was preached to you" (1 Peter 1:24–25).

But, I must admit, I am jealous of the access that some of these preachers have had into the White House. I would like to go just once. I know my sermon. I will preach from Acts 24, which recounts Paul before Felix and Drusilla. I will preach, as he did, concerning righteousness, self-control, and the judgment to come (cf. Acts 24:25). In doing this, I would expect to have my backside kicked quickly out the door! But if I were given such an opportunity, I would not go in and placate these powerful individuals with stories about nice men who are interested in God. After all, many nice men who are interested in God will go to hell. Herod was nice at times and interested in God; he liked to listen to John the Baptist preach. John's preaching might have set him going on a few things. He probably bought his wife flowers and tried to be nice to his mother-in-law for a while—clean up his act a little bit, get a little bit more religious. But he still put John the Baptist's head on a platter when it came to the crunch, because of the very immoral substance of his life. What he needed to hear was the message of the cross of Jesus Christ.

Let me come back to where I started. I said that the preaching of the cross was vital both for the believer and for the unbeliever. Let me give three points why the preaching of the cross is important for the unbeliever. First, it establishes the gravity of sin. Nowhere is the truth about sin more clearly stated than in the death of Jesus Christ. It is imperative that a person who is having the scales removed from his eyes by the Spirit of God sees in the cross the immensity of his offense. Suddenly, a verse like Romans 3:23—"All have sinned and come short of the glory of God"—begins to mean something when a person looks upon that cross. And when he has explained to him that Jesus Christ died on the cross because of that person's own sin—sin that put a cruel crown on Jesus' head and spit on him until it ran down his fair shoulders, sin that darkened the day at noon and caused that loud cry, "My God! My God! Why have you forsaken me?"—then, and only then, will men and women understand what all of it means.

Why is it that people are not crying to Christ for salvation? It is largely because we don't preach the cross. We explain the gospel in formulaic terms, but we miss the absolutely essential element of holding before the minds of our listeners this central emphasis. I say that to myself. I do not say it as someone who does it and wants to chide those who don't. I preach it first to my own heart. "The soul who sins shall die" (Ezek. 18:4). Men and women are perishing. While we believe that they are perishing cerebrally, we do not believe it viscerally. Jesus said, "Whoever believes in the Son has eternal life; whoever does not obey the Son shall not see life, but the wrath of God remains on him" (John 3:36). The only way that we can make that clear is to explain the cross, thereby bringing before the mind of the unbeliever the gravity of sin.

Second, the cross declares to the unbeliever the absolute necessity of grace. It is in the cross that all of God's mercy and the riches of his grace in the pardoning of sin are set forward. It is in the cross that we discover that although we are objects of wrath—who are disobedient, enslaved, and dead in our trespasses and our sins (cf. Eph. 2:1–2)—we become the objects of God's grace. This is because of the cross, the perfect propitiation.

In holding up the cross, we can look to Luke 15. Luke records how men and women are naturally lost in the story of the lost sheep, helplessly lost in the story of the lost coin, and willfully lost in the story of the lost son. When we have made that clear to people, where are they supposed to go when their hearts are gripped suddenly by the fact that they are lost? What should they do when the truth dawns on them and they say, "You know, I am like that coin, I am like that sheep, and that boy is me! I am in this city because the one thing I wanted was to get as far away as possible from parental constraint and restraint. I wanted money, freedom, and the opportunity to do my own thing. But here I am tonight, and the man has just described me!"? What do you say? Simply put, you tell them about the cross of the Lord Jesus Christ. It not only declares the gravity of sin but it also declares the absolute necessity of grace.

Either we preach that human beings are rebels against God— who are lost and under judgment and can only be saved by Christ bearing their sin on the cross—or we emphasize human potential and human ability, with Christ brought in only to boost them up! If we choose the latter, then there is no necessity for the cross except to exhibit God's love and to inspire us to greater endeavors. Sadly, that is largely the way the cross is proclaimed. Even sadder is the fact that many of the men who are doing it don't realize they are doing it. In this kind of preaching, the cross becomes a kind of additive to boost the enthusiasm of people's sparked religious interest. But what the cross conveys is the gravity of sin, our total inability to do anything at all, and the immensity and necessity of God's grace.

Third, the cross declares to the unbeliever the opportunity of faith. Isn't that what happened in Acts 2:36, after Peter preaches on the day of Pentecost and tells the crowd, "this Jesus whom you crucified has been made both Lord and Christ"? His hearers were cut to the heart. My fellow preachers, I hope you wish to preach and see somebody cut to the heart. To see somebody come up and say, "What do I do now?" We say to him or her, "Embrace the cross."

In conclusion, I want to say a word about why it is important to preach the cross to believers. First, because it gives to the believer a sense of compulsion. 2 Corinthians 5:14–15 says, "For the love of Christ controls [or compels] us, because we have concluded this: that one has died for all, therefore all have died; and he died for all, that those who live might no longer live for themselves but for him who for their sake died and was raised." Paul is saying, "The love of Christ constrains me and compels me; it drives me on for Christ." In effect, he is saying that Christ's love compels him and the other apostles because of what Jesus has done.

Those of us who believe our theological suppositions to be erudite must be about the business of weeping over the fallen and rescuing the perishing. We cannot write books on the cross of Christ that simply stoke our heads with information and fail to stir our hearts with the divine compulsion to see unbelieving people become committed followers of Jesus Christ. We must publish these books to stir up evangelistic activity and not merely increase theological ability.

Second, preaching the cross to the believer provides the necessary correction from reverting to the flesh after having begun in the Spirit (cf. Gal. 3:3). Paul asks the Galatians, "Are you so foolish? Having begun by the Spirit, are you now being perfected by the flesh?" The antidote to this kind of thinking is the preaching of the cross because it repeatedly brings the believer back to the essential truth. We preachers will see that in doing this Christ receives all the credit. He is the God who saves, and he is the God who keeps. I often think to myself, "What a mystery it is that after all these years—from the time I grasped the gospel in Sunday school and, at my father's chair, prayed to God to redeem me and bring me into the realm of his mercy—that here I am today. I may not be very far along but at least I am making progress." All credit goes to the cross of the Lord Jesus Christ. It compels me in evangelism, saves me, corrects my silly notions of struggling on, and it forms my character. A person who lives near the cross will be marked by holiness, love, and endurance.

Finally, we need to preach the cross to those who believe because there we find the basis for all of our confidence in living the Christian life. Isn't this what you find in Hebrews? "Therefore, brothers . . . we have confidence to enter the holy places by the blood of Jesus" (Heb. 10:19). What is the ground of our confidence when the Evil One comes to us and suddenly fires a fiery dart from out of left field? It happens constantly to us. It is some heinous thought; it may be a thought of jealousy.

It may be a thought of deep animosity. It may be an impure thought. Whatever it might be, in it comes, and it's there. And it is no sooner in your mind when "old smutty face," as C. S. Lewis called him, comes to the front door of your mind and says, "Hey! I thought you were a Christian! How could you possibly be a Christian and be thinking things like that?" What we normally say at this moment is, "Well, I know I was thinking that, but, you know, I read seventeen verses in my Bible this morning. Also, I was thinking about witnessing this afternoon." My friend, if you think like that, you are Islamic. You are trying to outweigh the bad with the good! Instead, you get to say, "Go back to hell where you belong." Beloved, in wearing the helmet of salvation, there is an awareness of the reality of the cross of Jesus Christ. We must find all of our confidence there. We must sing, with the old hymn writer,

Before the throne of God above,
I have a strong and perfect plea;
A great High Priest whose name is love,
Who ever lives and pleads for me.

When Satan tempts me to despair
And tells me of the guilt within,
Upward I look and see him there,
Who made an end to all my sin.

Because the sinless savior died.
My sinful soul is counted free
For God the just is satisfied
To look on him and pardon me.[1]

1. "Before the Throne of God Above." Words: Charitie L. Bancroft, 1863.

Index of Scripture

ALLIANCE®
OF CONFESSING EVANGELICALS

What is the Alliance?

The Alliance of Confessing Evangelicals is a coalition of Christian leaders from various denominations (Baptist, Presbyterian, Reformed, Congregational, Anglican, and Lutheran) committed to promoting a modern reformation of North America's church in doctrine, worship, and life, according to Scripture. We seek to call the twenty-first-century church to a modern reformation through broadcasting, events, publishing, and distribution of Reformed resources.

The work centers on broadcasting: *The Bible Study Hour* with James Boice, *Every Last Word* featuring Philip Ryken, *God's Living Word* with Bible teacher Richard Phillips, and *Dr. Barnhouse & the Bible* with Donald Barnhouse. These broadcasts air daily and weekly throughout North America as well as online and via satellite.

Our events include the Philadelphia Conference on Reformed Theology, the oldest continuing national Reformed conference in North America, and many regional events, including theology and exposition conferences and pastors' events, such as reformation societies that continue to join the hearts and minds of church leaders in pursuit of reformation in the church.

reformation21 is our online magazine—a free "go-to" theological resource. We also publish the *God's Word Today* online daily devotional; MatthewHenry.org, a source on biblical prayer; Alliance books from a list of diverse authors; and more.

The Alliance further seeks to encourage reformation in the church by offering a wide variety of CD and MP3 resources featuring Alliance broadcast speakers and many other nationally recognized pastors and theologians.